Christ Plays in Ten Thousand Places

STUDY GUIDE

Christ Plays in Ten Thousand Places

STUDY GUIDE

Eugene H. Peterson & Peter Santucci

WILLIAM B. EERDMANS PUBLISHING COMPANY

GRAND RAPIDS, MICHIGAN / CAMBRIDGE, U.K.

Wm. B. Eerdmans Publishing Co.
255 Jefferson Ave. S.E., Grand Rapids, Michigan 49503 /
P.O. Box 163, Cambridge CB3 9PU U.K.

Printed in the United States of America

10 09 08 07 06   7 6 5 4 3 2 1

ISBN-10 0-8028-3235-0
ISBN-13 978-0-8028-3235-1

www.eerdmans.com

Contents

CONTENTS

Contents

CONTENTS

Preface

Why a Study Guide?

Why is there a study guide to accompany *Christ Plays in Ten Thousand Places*? You already have Eugene Peterson's book, right? So, why add a book about the book written by someone you've never heard of? It's a good question. And I believe there are several very good answers to go with it.

The first answer is that one of Eugene Peterson's passions, which is expressed in both the book and his lifelong ministry as a pastor (and as a pastor to pastors), is to assure that what we know of God is actually and fully lived in the Christian community. Lived. Writing books and reading books just aren't enough. That's why the publisher has added this book to Eugene Peterson's book: To create conversations in which what we've read works its way deeper into who we are and finds expression in the way we actually live our lives.

The second answer is that another of Eugene Peterson's passions is to build community. It's easy to read books in isolation, taking things in, mulling them, chewing on them alone. It's easy to participate in our culture of self-help, adding a few more to-do items on our spiritual checklists to guarantee our progress up a sort of spiritual ladder. But Eugene Peterson will have nothing of that. God's desire for the nations, for the world — a community, not just a lump of individuals, for his name — is matched by Eugene Peterson's insistence that we're not ourselves when we're by ourselves, that the Christian life is only a Christian life when it is lived in community. Therefore, any reading and reflecting upon the Christian life ought to be done in community.

The third answer is that Eugene Peterson has been a teacher, mentor, and friend to me. And this is one way for the two of us to engage in "a conversation in spiritual theology," as the subtitle of the book suggests. While I studied at Regent College, I served Eugene Peterson and his students as a teaching assistant for several years. I read hundreds of papers as students responded to what he was teaching, and I sat in many classes, listening myself. Along with that, I've read almost everything Eugene Peterson has written for publication. In other words, he and I have been in conversation about the things in this book for many years. And this is our attempt to pull you into the conversation.

The fourth answer is my congregation. I used the several years after I left Regent to reimmerse myself in the workforce, working as the editor of a business magazine in Washington state. I didn't want to go straight from studying to pastoring. But now I am pastoring a wonderful bunch of saved sinners at First Presbyterian Church in Lebanon, Oregon, who are trying to meet Jesus and discover what real community and real worship and real life are like. This study guide is for them.

How to Use This Guide

Because *Christ Plays in Ten Thousand Places* was written as a book with just three long chapters, it wasn't easy at first to figure out how to present the book in a way that would work in a group setting. How could I break down the chapters into readable, discussable sections without losing the continuity of each chapter? I tried to keep each session's piece of the book to no more than thirty pages of reading — an amount that could be read in a sitting or two — while not breaking up the flow of the chapters too much. Eugene Peterson provided enough pauses and shifts in each chapter to make that possible. So, using thematic breaks and wanting to assign a reasonable number of pages to read for each session, I broke each of the three chapters into four parts:

- Part one of each chapter is Exploring the Neighborhood, which includes both *Kerygma* and Threat.

- Part two of each chapter is the first Grounding Text, the main Old Testament text for the chapter.
- Part three of each chapter is the second Grounding Text, the main New Testament text for the chapter.
- Part four of each chapter is Cultivating Fear-of-the-Lord, which includes the main way we participate in the action of God referred to in each chapter.

Groups wishing to speed things up a bit can easily group together parts as they see fit. For those wanting to do so, I'd recommend combining sessions 4 and 5, 8 and 9, and 12 and 13, pairing up the Old and New Testament grounding texts. Also, the two introductory sessions can be combined into one.

Each session has a summary of the section covered. I've included this for the sake of the group leader(s). You may or may not want to read this aloud before the group discussion. One problem with reading summaries aloud in small groups is that such summaries can lead to laziness, as when I was in eighth grade and read CliffsNotes on *Moby Dick* instead of the complete novel.

Along with questions for interaction, I've included quotations to consider. Eugene Peterson is eminently quotable, and I've had to restrain myself with the number of quotations included. (My wife was helpful in that process.) At times we need questions to spark our interaction, but at other times, simply reading a powerful and representative quotation is even more effective in generating interaction.

But remember, this guide includes a lot of quotations and questions. Make sure you consider the amount of time you have available for conversation and discussion before you pick which ones to use. Simply starting with the first quotation or the first question and trying to get through them all would be a mistake, unless you are using this guide for personal study. No group I know could have any depth of interaction while dealing with all the quotations and questions.

If you're using this study guide with a group that has been meeting together for a while, you probably have an established rhythm and way of interacting. If you're fairly new at this or are willing to explore a different shape for your time together, here is how our community groups operate (the groups I had in mind when I wrote this guide). It's fairly simple. We gather for a meal. The sharing of food makes it much easier to share our lives. Church-related talk is not permitted during meals. Talk about anything and everything else is encouraged. After the meal, we have our discussion time. Next, we take a break for dessert. And then we gather again for prayer. That's all. It's not a fool-proof technique, but it's a basic rhythm that makes sure that not only are we discussing the passage or book for that evening, but that we're also engaging each other as friends and praying for each other.

So, I encourage you to start each session with a meal together. And by the time you get to session 14, you'll feel like old pros at it.

What's in This Book

Many books come along that try to sell bundles, telling their wide-eyed Christian audiences the so-called secrets of the Christian life. For the most part, they offer a meager meal that quickly leaves us hungry and disappointed.

Eugene Peterson offers a multi-course feast, overflowing with flavors and colors. It takes time to digest such a meal. And not everything will agree with you. That's OK. Don't be discouraged.

One thing you'll notice is that Eugene Peterson doesn't say much about what we do as a Christian community. That's not because he's against our doing things. His aim is similar to that of St. Paul in 1 Corinthians — making sure the ground is cleared and the foundation well laid before the building goes up, so that what is built is strong, sound, and earthquake-proof. Too many of the books out there have us throwing up shiny shacks with no foundation or substance but that play on the desire of our egos to do something exciting and to get busy doing it now.

At times during your reading, therefore, you'll probably say, "That's great, but what do we do?" The answer is . . . keep doing what you're already doing. Just let this book help you reshape the reasons and the methods of your worshiping, praying, evangelizing, seeking justice, fellowshiping, and so on.

Remember, Christ plays in ten thousand places. The task of this book is not to be like a tourist guidebook pointing out those ten thousand places. It's up to you and your community to know your local "geography." Eugene Peterson's task is to remind us that it is Christ who is at play in us to the Father.

Preface

We get so focused on our Christian work, taking ourselves so seriously and working so hard that we forget that the most important thing has to do with Christ, not us, and with him playing, not us working. I hope the leisure with which he goes about playing in us to the Father will return the sparkle to our eyes and the lift to our step that we had when we first fell in love with Jesus.

Eugene Peterson puts first things first. What is first is not our working, but Christ's playing. His playing in and around us gives both shape and content to our doing.

Lebanon, Oregon PETER SANTUCCI
Summer 2005

Preface and Introduction

(pp. xi-xii and 1-9)

Unpacking the Poem

Early in the Introduction, Eugene Peterson quotes a poem by Gerard Manley Hopkins. For those unfamiliar with the poem, here it is in its entirety with a few comments to help you get inside it.

> As kingfishers catch fire, dragonflies draw flame;
>   As tumbled over rim in roundy wells
>   Stones ring; like each tucked string tells, each hung bell's
> Bow swung finds tongue to fling out broad its name;
> Each mortal thing does one thing and the same:
>   Deals out that being indoors each one dwells;
>   Selves — goes itself; *myself* it speaks and spells,
> Crying *What I do is me: for that I came.*
>
> I say more: the just man justices;
>   Keeps grace: that keeps all his goings graces;
> Acts in God's eye what in God's eye he is —
>   Christ — for Christ plays in ten thousand places,
> Lovely in limbs, and lovely in eyes not his
>   To the Father through the features of men's faces.

Notes on the Poem: The colors of kingfishers and dragonflies, the sounds made by stones and strings and bells — those are what these things were made for, those are the statements of who and what they are, those are their purposes. Humans, likewise, act as we were created to act: justly, graciously. But here's the amazing thing: The way we act is actually Christ playing through us and in us, playing "to the Father." Christ playing in us: That is what we were made for, that is our purpose, that is who we are. This is what Life is all about.

Summary

If a person's theology can be only thought or talked about, then it's not worthwhile, it's not true. If it's not livable, we're not interested. We need a lived spirituality.

At the same time, while we want to fully live who we are and what we believe, still more is going on than what fits into our day-in, day-out experience. There is More. There is God. We need a vibrant theology.

To live our lives fully with God, we need an adequate spiritual theology that takes in all of the details of our lives while always being shaped by the revelation of God in Scripture and in Jesus himself.

Key Terms

Spiritual theology: "the *lived* quality of God's revelation among and in us" (p. xi).

Spiritual: "the insistence that everything that God reveals of himself and his works is capable of being lived by ordinary men and women in their homes and workplaces" (p. 5).

Theology: "the attention we give to God, the effort we give to knowing God as revealed in the Holy Scriptures and in Jesus Christ" (p. 5).

Quotations to Consider

"The end of all Christian belief and obedience, witness and teaching, marriage and family, leisure and work life, preaching and pastoral work is the living of everything we know about God: life, life, and more life" (p. 1).

"'Spiritual' keeps 'theology' from degenerating into merely thinking and talking and writing about God at a distance. . . . We know how easy it is for us to let our story of God (theology) get separated from the way we live" (p. 5).

"'Theology' keeps 'spiritual' from becoming merely thinking and talking and writing about the feelings and thoughts one has about God. . . . We know how easy it is to let our desires to live whole and satisfying lives (spiritual lives) get disconnected from who God actually is and the ways he works among us" (p. 5).

". . . we do not know God by defining him but by being loved by him and loving in return" (p. 7).

Questions for Interaction

1. In his poem, Gerard Manley Hopkins writes, "Christ plays in ten thousand places,/Lovely in limbs, and lovely in eyes not his/To the Father through the features of men's faces." Why does the idea of Christ playing likely feel foreign to you? What makes or would make your life feel like a place where Christ would want to play? How does the idea of Christ playing in you change the way you think about and act toward yourself? How about the ways you think about and act toward others in whom he is playing?

2. How do you respond to the word "spirituality"? Is it a word that draws you in or that makes you draw back? Why does it do so?

3. How do you respond to the word "theology"? Is it a word that causes your mind to open up or shut down? Why do you respond in this way?

4. "Spiritual" and "ordinary" are rarely equated. In fact, they're often considered opposites. What makes you think Eugene correct or not correct in equating them? How does equating them change the way you approach the boring, mundane, messy, routine parts of your life? Of the lives of other people? How much of what is spiritual have you been missing out on?

5. Eugene Peterson writes that ". . . everything about us . . . takes place in the 'country' of the Trinity . . ." (p. 6). How vague or foreign an idea is "Trinity" to you? Or how does it shape the way you approach

God and your own life? What might it mean to live in the "country" of the Trinity?

Prayers

David Adam has collected prayers from the Celtic tradition in a series of books. One of the hallmarks of Celtic spirituality is its adamant refusal to separate the spiritual from the ordinary. One prayer from Adam's book *The Edge of Glory: Prayers in the Celtic Tradition* (SPCK, 1985, p. 29) is one that would be prayed during the mundane task of digging holes. It begins with the line, "All that I dig with the spade, I do it with my Father's aid." It continues through each Person of the Trinity, ending with a declaration that all is done for the sake of the Trinity.

Try using the basic shape of this prayer to pray for and in some of your basic daily tasks — changing diapers, washing the car, taking out the trash, paying the bills, you name it. Report back to the group on how praying the details of your week shaped you during the week. How easy or difficult was it for you to remember to pray the details as you were in the midst of them?

Clearing the Playing Field

(pp. 11-47)

Summary

Although "spirituality" seems quite alive these days with all the attention it gets, this popular view of spirituality has some basic problems. First, it is generally elitist. Second, it wanders from our basic text, the Bible. Third, it becomes emptied of any gospel distinctives. And finally, it ends up jettisoning theology and most of God with it.

Our goal is to pull from the energy in contemporary spiritualities while restoring the biblical shape with Christ as its center. The back-to-back stories of Nicodemus and the Samaritan woman (John 3–4) establish the parameters for participation: Everyone can participate. "The God-breathed life is common, it is totally accessible across the whole spectrum of the human condition. We are welcomed into life, period. There are no pre-conditions" (p. 17). By pairing these stories, John's Gospel takes the first step in erasing any sort of elitism that might creep in.

Eugene Peterson points to the importance of the Spirit of God in the stories of both Nicodemus and the Samaritan woman. "In both conversations 'spirit' is the pivotal word" (p. 18). "It is only because God is Spirit that there is anything to say about what we do and don't do" (p. 19). Spirit is the context for our spirit-uality.

At the same time, "Jesus is the primary figure in both stories. Jesus is far more active than any one of us; it is Jesus who provides the energy" (p. 19). Not only are these stories more about Jesus than about Nicodemus and a Samaritan woman, but likewise our lives are more about Jesus than about us.

Eugene Peterson makes three ground-clearing observations: "[S]pirituality is not a body of secret lore, spirituality has nothing to do with aptitude or temperament, spirituality is not primarily about you or me; it is not about personal power or enrichment. It is about God" (p. 19).

Although "life" is the main word of creation, death keeps finding its way in. But creation doesn't stop with the initial burst way back when. Creation and re-creation are God's on-going actions, countering death and breathing life again and again. The Spirit of God is always creating in and around us.

Rather than using "spirituality" as a specialized term to designate extraordinary holiness, Eugene Peterson prefers to use the word to mark any activity of God's Spirit in our lives, no matter how ordinary and mundane. He calls it an "organic linkage to this Beyond and Within that are part of everyone's experience" (p. 27).

Abstraction is crippling to authentic spirituality. Real spirituality is tied to creation, not to terms, ideas, and feelings. Spirituality has just as much to do with the material, external, and visible as it does with the immaterial, internal, and invisible. What it has nothing to do with is death, including those things that kill by depersonalizing, functionalizing, and psychologizing us.

To keep our culture from reducing us to mere objects and killing the Spirit, we need vigilance and attentiveness. We maintain vigilance by continually and carefully reading Holy Scripture, and we nurture attentiveness through common worship and personal prayer.

Jesus is the focal point of all Christian spirituality. He reveals God to us and does so in the nameable, datable, geographically locatable details of life. His very physical humanness keeps us safe from abstracted anti-spiritualities.

"Jesus tells us everything we need to know about God" (p. 32). And yet many of the details of his life are left out — we're given what we need, not what we're curious about. Other, non-biblical writers have tried to give us extra details, but none of them have been helpful.

Our soul, "the totality of what it means to be a human being" (p. 36), makes us unique and fit for God. On the other hand, "Self is the soul minus God" (p. 37). Our soulless culture knows nothing of the soul and everything of the self, turning us into either consumers or problems.

We are reduced to being "resources" for others to use or machines that are either functional or dysfunctional, neither of which reduction is personal or human, neither of which has a soul.

We get in on what God is doing through fear-of-the-Lord. This has nothing to do with being afraid of God. Rather, it has to do with living in reverence before what God does and responding appropriately in the way of Jesus.

Essential to living in the way of God is living in the context of the Trinity. As Trinity, God is always relational. An image of this relationship is expressed in the Greek word *perichoresis,* which simply means "circle dance." In other words, the relationship is not static, but always in motion, as each member moves with and around the others in a joyful dance. The Christian life allows for no mere spectators to this life of God but pulls us in as participants in the dance.

Key Terms

Spirituality: another way of referring to the Christian life; ". . . a serious and disciplined commitment to live deeply and fully in relation to God"; ". . . transcendence vaguely intermingled with intimacy"; ". . . the catch-all term that recognizes an organic linkage to this Beyond and Within that are part of everyone's experience"; ". . . a term that covers the waterfront . . ." (p. 27).

Transcendence: "a sense that there is more, a sense that life extends far beyond me . . ." (p. 27).

Idolatry: "reducing God to a concept or object that we can use for our benefit" (p. 29); abstraction is the beginning of idolatry.

Holy Spirit: "God's living presence at work among us" (p. 20).

Soul: "the core being of men and women" (p. 36); our one-of-a-kind, image-of-God, persons-in-relationship identity which defies reduction; the opposite of "self," which is the "soul minus God" (p. 37).

Fear-of-the-Lord: a single, bound-together word for the way the Christian life is lived, a way that is dominated by an awareness of who God is and the way God acts — "the way of life that is lived responsively and appropriately before who God is, who he is as Father, Son, and Holy Spirit" (p. 40); "a way of life in which human feelings and behavior are fused with God's being and revelation" (p. 42); "the way of life appropriate to our creation and salvation and blessing by God" (p. 43).

Perichoresis: a Greek word for dance (*peri* = around; *choresis* = dance) used as an image of the way the Persons of the Trinity — Father, Son, Spirit — interact with each other.

Quotations to Consider

"Stories are verbal acts of hospitality" (p. 13).

"'Create' is not confined to what the Spirit did; it is what the Spirit *does*" (p. 22).

"Biblically, we are given an extensively narrated story of life assaulted by death but all the time surviving death, with God constantly, in new ways and old, breathing life into this death-plagued creation, these death-battered lives. A complex plot emerges as we read this story: God creating a way of life out of this chaos and misery, God countering death, God breathing life into creation and creatures and the life-breath becoming audible in language over and over again" (p. 24).

". . . reality is *spoken* into being" (p. 26).

"For most people [the word "spirituality"] conveys no sense of the life of God: *Spirit* of God, *Spirit* of Christ, Holy *Spirit*. The more the word is secularized the less useful it is" (p. 29).

"Idolatry, reducing God to a concept or object that we can use for our benefit, is endemic to the human condition" (pp. 29-30).

"Jesus is the central and defining figure in the spiritual life. His life is, precisely, *revelation*. He brings out into the open what we could never have figured out for ourselves, never guessed in a million years" (p. 31).

"By accepting Jesus as the final and definitive revelation of God, the Christian church makes it impossible for us to make up our own customized variations of the spiritual life and get away with it, not that we don't try" (p. 33).

"Jesus insists that we deal with God right here and now, in the place we find ourselves and with the people we are with. Jesus *is* God here and now" (p. 34).

"The ordinariness of Jesus was a huge roadblock to belief in his identity and work in the 'days of his flesh.' It is still a roadblock" (p. 35).

"When it comes to dealing with God, most of us spend considerable time trying our own hands at either being or making gods. Jesus blocks the way. Jesus is not a god of our own making and he is certainly not a god designed to win popularity contests" (p. 36).

"The term 'soul' works like a magnet, pulling all the pieces of our lives into a unity, a totality. The human person is a vast totality; 'soul' names it as such" (p. 37).

"We live in a culture that has replaced soul with self. This reduction turns people either into problems or consumers. . . . [E]veryone we meet is either a potential recruit to join our enterprise or a potential consumer for what we are selling; or we ourselves are the potential recruits and consumers" (p. 38).

"Widespread consumerism results in extensive depersonalization. And every time depersonalization moves in, life leaks out" (p. 39).

"The moment we find ourselves unexpectedly in the presence of the sacred, our first response is to stop in silence. We do nothing. We say nothing" (p. 41).

"Human beings are not gods; the moment we forget this, we violate the boundaries of our humanity and something is violated in reality itself. The universe suffers damage" (p. 42).

"Fear-of-the-Lord is not studying about God but living in reverence before God. We don't so much lack knowledge, we lack reverence. Fear-of-the-Lord is not a technique for acquiring spiritual know-how but a willed not-knowing. . . . Fear-of-the-Lord, nurtured in worship and prayer, silence and quiet, love and sacrifice, turns everything we do into a life of 'breathing God'" (p. 44).

"It is the easiest thing in the world to use words as a kind of abstract truth or principle, to deal with the gospel as information. Trinity prevents us from doing this" (p. 45).

"Knowing God through impersonal abstractions is ruled out, knowing God through programmatic projects is abandoned, knowing God in solitary isolation is forbidden. Trinity insists that God is not an idea or a force or a private experience but personal and known only in personal response and engagement" (p. 46).

"God is never a commodity to use" (p. 46).

"It is the participation in the Trinity (God as he has revealed himself to us) that makes things and people particularly and distinctively who they are. We are not spectators to God; there is always a hand reaching out to pull us into the Trinitarian actions of holy creation, holy salvation, and holy community. God is never a nonparticipant in what he does, nor are any of us. There are no nonparticipants in a Trinity-revealed life" (p. 46).

"If we are going to know God we have to participate in the relationship that is God" (p. 46).

Questions for Interaction

1. How does thinking of God as the creator and yourself as a sub-creator shape the way you approach the things you do?
2. Read aloud the three passages referred to — Genesis 1:1-3; Mark 1:9-11; Acts 2:1-3. In them, the Spirit prepares for and energizes three acts of creation: the heavens and the earth; the ministry of Jesus; and the church. List similarities and differences among the three passages. Would you agree that the Spirit of God is hovering over and creating/re-creating your church? Your life? How is that manifest? What manifestations of the Spirit's creative work are others in the group seeing that you aren't?
3. Rather than using "spirituality" as a specialized term to designate extraordinary holiness, Eugene Peterson prefers to use the word to mark any activity of God's Spirit in our lives, no matter how ordinary and mundane. Do you divide your life and the world around you into parts that are spiritual and parts that are not spiritual?

What might you be missing out on in this chopped-up approach to yourself and the world?

4. Abstraction is crippling to authentic spirituality. Real spirituality is tied to creation, not to terms, ideas, and feelings. How does the world turn people into abstractions (numbers, target markets, head count, etc.)? In what ways has this drifted into churches? How might you be able to reverse this trend?

5. "Jesus insists that we deal with God right here and now, in the place we find ourselves and with the people we are with" (p. 34). Have you ever wished you were part of a different family or marriage or church, thinking that your life would somehow be different and better? How does the detailed life of Jesus pop that bubble? How does his life restore our connections with our often unpleasant context and relationships?

6. The term *perichoresis* describes the Trinity — always in a motion, each Person dancing with and around the others. A photo of a dance kills it, stopping all motion and fixing each dancer in one spot. Is your image of God one that is in motion or one that could be captured in a snapshot? How do you react to the image of God dancing? How does it change the way you approach God? What would it be like for you to join the dance? What about your church?

Prayers

The English poet Christina Rossetti (1830-1894) wrote a simple prayer that gets at what Eugene Peterson is emphasizing in his discussion of the focal practice of the fear-of-the-Lord. Use it as an entry into your time of prayer.

"Teach us, O Lord, to fear you without being afraid; to fear you in love that we may love you without fear."

Christ Plays in Creation (1)

(pp. 49-62)

Summary

Before we are "born again," we are simply born. We are alive. Life is the most basic reality of our, well, lives. Bursting with life, we live in the theater of creation.

But creation is more than just the natural world. It is what God does. God creates. So, we enter into creation not just by birth, but by belief, belief in God the Creator.

The Greek word *kerygma* means "a public proclamation that brings what it proclaims into historical reality" (p. 53). In other words, speaking something into being. Telling the story of Jesus' birth — which is itself a "creation" story — has the (kerygmatic) effect of drawing us into and enabling us to participate in creation. Speaking about his participation creates ours.

In an era of birth control and fertility drugs and procedures, we have a strong sense of planning and control in conception and later in birth. But Scripture boldly proclaims something our modern minds reel at: a virgin birth. And not only that, but five other miracle births. They pop the bubble of our sense of control and return us to a state of wonder.

But the messiness of children has always annoyed abstract spiritual purists. They haven't been thrilled with the humanity of Jesus either. Wanting only sublime truths, many have tried to smooth Jesus over and universalize him as the teacher of the secrets of God. "'Gnostic' is the term we often use to designate this most attractive but soul-destroying spirituality" (p. 61).

Although there was never an official gnostic religion, it quickly attached itself like a parasite to Christianity. It has five basic beliefs: (1) the physical creation isn't good; (2) a secret "knowledge (gnosis) . . . can save us from this hopeless condition" (p. 61); (3) escaping creation (and its God) and/or the sinful world is a basic strategy; (4) you're better than the rest, because of what you know; and (5) you're the final authority on what is true and how best to live.

According to biblical faith, all of life is spiritual and everything we do has to do with God, but gnostics would exclude the physical from the spiritual. By excluding much of life from having any spiritual significance, gnostics tend to live out of balance, spending too much or too little attention on the details of their lives.

Key Terms

Kerygma: "a public proclamation that brings what it proclaims into historical reality" (p. 53); in other words, speaking something into being.

Gnosticism: a belief that (1) the physical creation isn't good; (2) a secret "knowledge (gnosis) . . . can save us from this hopeless condition" (p. 61); (3) escaping creation (and its God) and/or the sinful world is a basic strategy; (4) you're better than the rest, because of what you know; and (5) you're the final authority on what is true and how best to live.

Quotations to Consider

"We wake up each morning to a world we did not make" (p. 51).

"After awhile we get used to it and quit noticing" (p. 51).

"Creation is not something we figure out, or deduce, or argue, or simply appreciate as is — it is what we believe: *credo*" (p. 52).

"We are not spectators of creation but participants in it" (p. 54).

"The Christian life is the practice of living in what God has done and is doing" (p. 54).

"But every birth can, if we let it, return us to the wonder of Jesus' birth, the revelation of sheer life as gift, God's life with us and for us" (p. 57).

"God himself is personally present and totally participant in creation, which is good news indeed" (p. 59).

"We imagine that we were created for higher things, that there is a world of subtle ideas and fine feelings and exquisite ecstasies for us to cultivate" (p. 59).

"Gnosticism offers us spirituality without the inconvenience of creation . . . of sin or morality . . . of people who we don't like or who aren't 'our kind'" (p. 62).

Questions for Interaction

1. Have you ever felt the desire for creation without the mess of people — the desire to "get away from it all," ditching friends, family, church, job, and get out into a wide open space? What's right with this reaction? What's wrong with it?
2. What grabs you most in the birth story of Jesus: The heavenly majesty of the angels and dreams, royal visitors and royal genealogies? Or the earthy details of shepherds and sheep shacks, unwed motherhood and the birthing process? How do the stories hold the heavenly majesty and the earthy details together?
3. Jesus' birth is told as a "creation" story. How does that change the way you read it and respond to it?
4. How do the virgin birth of Jesus and the five other miraculous births in Scripture restore a sense of wonder to our modern, technologized process of conception and of giving life?
5. The messiness of raising children often obscures the wonder of birth and the creation of new life. When you're around children (your own or those of others) do you find yourself more in awe of the created life or annoyed by the chaotic mess? Why?
6. In what ways have you given in to the lures of gnosticism? Have you

ever studied books, programs, or teachers who offered "secrets" of the spiritual life? How did the "secrets" pan out?

7. Are you more comfortable with a Christ who is fully God or a Jesus who is fully human? What about his crude humanness makes you uncomfortable?

8. According to biblical faith, all of life is spiritual and everything we do has to do with God, but by excluding much of physical life from having any spiritual significance, gnostics tend to live out of balance, spending too much or too little attention on the details of their lives. Which parts of your life do you tend to ignore? What parts of your life do you tend to indulge?

9. How does American culture encourage a gnostic approach to life?

Prayers

My three-year-old son, Josiah, flirted with gnosticism during his meal prayers ("Thank you, God, for everything") but is now blessed with the gift of particularity in both his meal prayers ("Thank you, God, for the salt and the pepper and spoons and forks and . . .") and night prayers ("Thank you, God, for Hannah and Eli and Kayla and Owen and . . ."). Taking a page out of his book, close your eyes and hold your hands out in front of yourself, lifting them up to God. Recall and name aloud at least twenty people. Then think of and name aloud at least twenty specific physical things.

SESSION 4

Christ Plays in Creation (2)

(pp. 62-85)

Summary

Our contemporary "cultural and spiritual conditions" match "the exile conditions of the Hebrews in the sixth century before Christ: the pervasive uprootedness and loss of place, the loss of connection with a tradition of worship, the sense of being immersed in a foreign and idolatrous society" (p. 64).

All our lives have "Sister Lychens" (pp. 65-67) who live anti-creation lives, ignoring creation and seeking to escape it in different ways.

The first biblical creation account establishes the rhythmic backbeat to creation. The second account "is more like a story with a setting in place where a plot begins to form and characters are introduced" (p. 72).

The basic way to enter into a spirituality of creation is by joining in the rhythm of creation — "the steady, sure, unhurried pace of God" (p. 71). Worship ought to reconnect us with these creation rhythms instead of disconnecting us from them.

A spirituality of creation ties us to a particular place. We all have addresses; we all have our place. None of these places, however, meet our expectations, and we're tempted to engage in the building of utopias. But these perfect places are no-places. Against the gnosticism of utopian fantasies, biblical faith roots us in an actual place and tells us, "Stay. Be faithful here." Scripture refuses to sanction our desire to escape our relationships and our conditions of life. "God works with us as we are and not as we should be or think we should be" (p. 75).

16

To be human is to be humus, the dirt we were created from. As such, we are to be humble and tied to the stuff we're made of. What is around us isn't our "environment," it is the same "creation" that we are part of ourselves. But we're more than dirt. God has given us a dignified place. God has invited us to participate in and continue his work, under his guidance. Our first job is conservation, taking care of God's good earth. Amazingly, along with a job, God gives us the freedom to say No to him, to obey or disobey. This freedom is essential to our humanity. But freedom is also matched with necessity.

Naming invites intimacy. It invites a personal form of knowing, though it doesn't guarantee intimacy. A relational answer is required for the intimacy we were created for.

Key Terms

Hurry: "Hurry turns away from the gift of time in a compulsive grasping for abstractions that it can possess and control" (p. 65).

Procrastination: "Procrastination is distracted from the gift of time in a lazy inattentiveness to the life of obedience and adoration by which we enter the 'fullness of time'" (p. 65).

Quotations to Consider

"Men and women don't, *can't*, create. But God does. . . . When the conditions in which we live seem totally alien to life and salvation, we are reduced to waiting for God to do what only God can do, create" (p. 64).

"The end time is not a future we wait for but the gift of the fullness of time that we receive in adoration and obedience as it flows into the present" (p. 67).

"Worship is the primary means for forming us as participants in God's work, but if the blinds are drawn while we wait for Sunday, we aren't in touch with the work that God is actually doing" (p. 71).

"One of the seductions that bedevils Christian formation is the construction of utopias, ideal places where we can live totally and without inhibition or interference the good and blessed and righteous life" (p. 73).

"What we often consider to be the concerns of the spiritual life — ideas, truths, prayers, promises, beliefs — are never in the Christian gospel permitted to have a life of their own apart from particular persons and actual places. Biblical spirituality/religion has a low tolerance for 'great ideas' or 'sublime truths' or 'inspirational thoughts' apart from the people and places in which they occur. God's great love and purposes for us are all worked out in messes in our kitchens and backyards, in storms and sins, blue skies, the daily work and dreams of our common lives" (p. 75).

Creation ". . . is not something apart from us; it is part of us and we are part of it" (p. 76).

"The Latin words *humus,* soil/earth, and *homo,* human being, have a common derivation, from which we also get our word 'humble.' This is the Genesis origin of who we are: dust — dust that the Lord God used to make us a human being. If we cultivate a lively sense of our origin and nurture a sense of continuity with it, who knows, we may also acquire humility" (p. 76).

"The gospel of Jesus Christ has no patience with a spirituality that is general or abstract, that is all ideas and feelings, and that takes as its theme song, 'This world is not my home, I'm just a-passing through.' Theology divorced from geography gets us into nothing but trouble" (p. 77).

"Conservation of the place in which we live is the first work assignment that occurs in our Scriptures" (p. 78).

"Freedom does not mean doing whatever pops into our heads. . . . Freedom and necessity are twinned realities. Much of the art of living consists in acquiring skill in negotiating with them" (p. 79).

"If we slight necessity, our so-called freedom is nothing but blundering and flailing about, maiming ourselves and others, whether morally or physically — usually both. If we slight freedom, submitting passivity to necessity, we become sluggish, forfeit the unique particularity of our humanness, and sink into the parasitic state of consumer and spectator" (p. 79).

"Naming identifies. Naming, when done well, captures something of the essence of the life so named" (p. 80).

"We are not disembodied angels. We have a street address where God can find us" (pp. 84-85).

"A primary but often shirked task of the Christian in our society and culture is to notice, to see in detail, the sacredness of creation. The marks of God's creative work are all around and in us" (p. 85).

Questions for Interaction

1. "All living is local" (p. 72). How many of your neighbors do you know? What are the colors of the houses (and/or other buildings) on your street? What do you pass by on your way to work? What are the names of your bank teller and grocery store clerk? How many of the close-to-home details of your life are you passing over with regularity?

2. Only God creates. We can't. Does this make you feel helpless or hopeful? How so?

3. Sister Lychen turned the Christian life from one of participating in creation into one of ignoring the world at best and seeking to escape it at worst. Do you have any stories of your own Sister Lychen? When have you been a Sister Lychen?

4. Many people speak of wanting "balance" in their lives, but Eugene Peterson points to rhythm. What is the difference? Which is easier: a juggler keeping ten balls in "balance" or ten musicians playing to one rhythm?

5. Have you ever left a job because you weren't meeting your potential? Or left a church because it didn't meet your standards? Or left a marriage because it was dragging you down? Tell about one of these leave-takings. Have you ever been in a less-than-ideal situation and chosen to stay, to stick it out?

6. Think about the people and the details that you would erase from your life if you could. With them in mind, consider this statement: "God deals with us where we are and not where we would like to be" (p. 75). How are these details and people an essential part of how God is dealing with you?

7. How does the word "environment" put a distance between us and the world around us that the word "creation" doesn't, since we are

ourselves creatures, God's creation? How tied to the life and health of the rest of creation around you do you feel? How does that connection shape the way you live?

8. How do you hold freedom and necessity in tension in your life? Which way do you lean? Do you tend to dangerously throw off necessities for the sake of freedom or do you tend to give up your freedom for the sake of necessity?

9. What danger is there in not seeing other humans as creatures, as part of the creation? How is this dangerous in our approach to the non-human creation as well?

Prayers

Use the following excerpt from one of the sermons of St. Augustine (354-430) as a guide to your named, particular, placed prayers, shaped by the life of Jesus.

> The Word of the Father, by whom all the cycles of time were made,
>   when he was made flesh, caused the day of his birth
>   to take place in time. . . .
> With the Father, he preceded all the ages of the world;
>   by the mother, he set himself on this day in the courses
>   of the years.
> The Maker was made man,
> That the Ruler of the stars might suck at the breast;
> That the Bread might be hungered;
> The Fountain, thirst;
> The Light, sleep;
> The Way, be wearied by the journey;
> The Truth, be accused by false witnesses;
> The Judge of the living and the dead, be judged by a mortal judge;
> The Chastener, be chastened with whips;
> The Vine, be crowned with thorns;
> The Foundation, be hung upon a tree;
> Strength, be made weak;
> Health, be wounded;
> Life, die.

Christ Plays in Creation (3)

(pp. 85-108)

Summary

In John's Gospel, we see Jesus engaging in conversation after conversation, engaging in person-to-person communication. Jesus is not shown just as a functional savior, but as a relational person. When he speaks, God speaks. In Jesus, the God who had spoken in the Old Testament speaks again, but with a human face and in personal conversation. And there is an intimacy and leisure to the way he goes about it.

Contrary to how they're often used, the "signs" in John's Gospel are not meant to impress and are "not for advertising or entertainment" (p. 92). They are meant "to give us a look into the creation instead of just at it" (p. 92), to give us a look into Jesus instead of just at him.

These miracles also point to the unforced nature of belief. They are merely signposts, hopefully leading to faith in Jesus, but they cannot create or coerce faith in anyone. Jesus' word, not the signs, forms belief. At times, a sign actually draws our murderous hostility, the polar opposite of belief. And just as Jesus doesn't coerce belief in us with his signs, he himself will not be coerced, taken over by our agenda for him, our requirement of signs from him.

"Glory" is a key term in John's Gospel. It's a word associated with the brilliance, weight, and honor of the revealed presence of God, with seeing a glimpse of God. Jews at that time expected that God's presence would return to the temple in Jerusalem with glory. But John says, in effect, "We saw the Glory. It was Jesus who was God right here among us."

But not only that, John ties the death of Jesus on the cross to the moment of glorification, the revealing of the glory of God in its greatest splendor.

Jesus has completely redefined glory by going through the worst of things instead of the best of things in his glorification. We get in on the Jesus kind of glory by dying, too. And, Eugene Peterson notes, "Christians don't have to wait until we die to die." Christian spirituality is marked by a letting go, a dying to self that participates in the glory of Jesus.

Key Terms

Egō eimi: Greek for "I am." "I am" is the "most personal name for God in the Scriptures" (p. 89) and is used by Jesus in John's Gospel as he takes the divine Name as his own.

Signs: The supernatural phenomena and marvels that Jesus performed, which pointed to who he really is as the Word made flesh. Often missed or misunderstood, they are of limited value. Their main value is in showing God still at his creation work in Jesus.

Glory: ". . . the extravagant brightness that marks God's presence among us" (p. 99). Its use in the Hebrew Bible is tied to the "weight" or significance of things.

Shekinah: The noun form of the Hebrew verb "to dwell." It was "widely used in the Hebrew religious community to mark God's presence, God dwelling among his people accompanied by a visible display of bright glory" (p. 100).

Quotations to Consider

"The Gospel of John is the creation story with Jesus Christ presented as simultaneously the revelation of Creator and creation" (p. 85).

"It is not uncommon among people like us to suppose that if we lived in another place or a better neighborhood with more congenial living conditions, voted in a better government, built finer schools, then we would most certainly live a more spiritual life. St. John's Gospel says, Forget it" (p. 86).

"Jesus in this story not only speaks the word of God; he is the Word of God" (p. 87).

"Keeping company with Jesus we become insiders to the creation. It is not something 'out there' that we can adopt or ignore as we will. . . . We are embedded in the creation, we are integral to the creation" (p. 87).

John "is not nearly as interested in telling us anything new *about* Jesus . . . as he is in drawing us into an increasingly intimate relationship *with* Jesus" (p. 91).

"The miraculous is no proof of truth or reality. Supernatural marvels have wonderful entertainment value, but not much else" (p. 92).

"Jesus has no time for people who demand the sensational to validate truth or confirm God's presence among them" (p. 93).

". . . we cannot be *made* to believe. Belief by its very nature requires assent and participation, trust and commitment. When we believe we are at our most personal and intimate with another, with the Other. Belief cannot be forced" (pp. 93-94).

"Signs reveal Jesus as God at work among us, but they also reveal how unready so many of us are to accept and embrace what is revealed and how contentious we can become when the God in heaven that we worship turns out to be involved in the details of our daily lives on this earth in ways that don't fit our preconceptions" (p. 96).

"We have such stereotyped ideas of what God does and how he does it that we frequently misread the signposts. As John makes us insiders to these seven named signs, we realize how often in our preoccupation with our self-importance we miss seeing what is going on right under our eyes . . . ; how, with our fixed idea of how God works, we dismiss what is overwhelmingly obvious . . . ; how, in a flush of blessings, we try to grab Jesus and enlist him for our personal agendas . . . ; how easily and quickly devastation or death or its emotional and circumstantial equivalent . . . pushes Jesus out of the center to the margins while we get on the best we can with what we have: courage and resignation . . . , accusation and weeping . . . , or retaliation even to the extent of murder . . ." (pp. 97-98).

"'Glory' is the light-filled word spilling out the extravagant brightness that marks God's presence among us" (p. 99).

"Nothing of the splendor that is conveyed in [the] earlier expressions of the glory is to be dismissed or minimized in any way. But this glory must now be reimagined and received and entered into as Jesus reveals it: Jesus ignorable, Jesus unimpressive, Jesus dismissed, Jesus marginalized, Jesus suffering, Jesus rejected, Jesus derided, Jesus hung on a cross, and — the final and irrefutable indignity — Jesus dead and buried. All this is included in the content of 'we beheld his glory'" (p. 101).

"Jesus takes the brightest word in our vocabularies and plunges it into the darkest pit of experience, violent and excruciating death. Everything we ever associated with glory has to be recast: We have entered a mystery" (p. 102).

"Christians don't have to wait until we die to die. We don't have to wait until our funerals to get in on the glory" (p. 103).

"When we believe, we respond embracingly to what we cannot see, the things of heaven. Belief is worked out in a life of worship and prayer to God, Father, Son, and Holy Spirit. When we love, we respond embracingly to what we can see and touch and hear, the things of earth. Love is worked out in lives of intimacy and care among the people in our families and neighborhoods and workplaces" (pp. 107-8).

"Things, stuff, bodies are holy. As we think and act sacramentally we learn to believe" (p. 108).

Questions for Interaction

1. In John's Gospel, we see Jesus engaging in conversations. How does this relational presentation of Jesus affect the way you approach him yourself? How does it affect the way you approach others?
2. People often try to manipulate and control God. What are some of the things that you want to take place that God is just not performing for you? What signs, if any, would you like God to perform?
3. Belief finds its goal in worship. Is communal worship a part of your regular practice? How does this influence your belief?
4. How does the world around us define "glory"? What are the main ingredients in achieving glory in our culture?
5. John's Gospel ties the glory of Jesus with his death. How does this

redefine glory? How does this redefine death (and particularly Jesus' death)?

6. Eugene Peterson refers to spiritual "tourists" who seem like seekers but aren't interested in any sort of real depth. They dabble in Jesus but not in the cross. What is the danger in being a spiritual tourist? What is the danger in trying to appeal to tourists?

7. We get in on the Jesus kind of glory by dying, too. And, Eugene Peterson notes, "Christians don't have to wait until we die to die." What will it take for you to get in on the Jesus kind of glory? What kind of dying is God requiring of you?

8. "Things, stuff, bodies are holy." How do our bodies and the stuff of the world we live in show us the glory of God? How do they help us lead lives of belief and love?

Prayers

Use the seven "I am" sayings of Jesus to shape your praying together —

> I am the bread of life;
> I am the light of the world;
> I am the gate;
> I am the good shepherd;
> I am the resurrection and the life;
> I am the way, the truth, and the life;
> I am the vine.

As you pray, consider how God has revealed himself to you in similar tangible ways.

Christ Plays in Creation (4)

(pp. 108-29)

Summary

Sabbath-keeping is the focal practice of a creation spirituality, giving concrete expression to something that could easily slip into useless abstraction. We get in on what God is doing in creation by keeping the Sabbath: We start by stopping.

In order to get our work right, we have to pay attention to God and his work. Sabbath gives us pause from our work just long enough to notice and attend to God and his work.

Entering a place of worship, not taking up the bird-watching glasses or some other type of "communion" with nature, is the best way to embed Sabbath-keeping into our lives. Sunday worship restores our bearings for the rest of the week, making us "adept at discerning the Jesus-signs and picking up on the Jesus-words that reveal the presence and the glory. We are more deeply at home in the creation than ever" (p. 113).

God works and God rests. Work and Sabbath go together. "Either apart from the other is crippled" (p. 115).

Because we operate out of our strengths and can do amazing things, in our work we are all at our most god-like. And we are most at risk of idolatry. By taking a break from our work and spending the day remembering the Creator, we take the air out of our idolatry and attend to God again.

Sabbath-keeping helps us restore wonder to our lives. In our scientific, figured-out world, we need to remember that we don't know all that much. In our world of experts, we need to remember that we're still and always will be beginners. In our world of celebrities, we need to see the marginalized. In our world of noise and glitz, we need to look for the quiet and unassuming. In a world of assumptions, we need to be ready for anything. All of these are aspects of a restored wonder.

When we lose our wonder, we become motivated by our anxiety and guilt. We grasp for control from God and then, ironically, ask (and even command) God to help us out. Instead of watching in wonder as God works, we wonder why God isn't helping us do his work for him. This movement from worshiping God to using God is the road to idolatry.

Whenever spirituality becomes a consumer product, we end up packaging God and reducing him to an idol. Whenever our identities are formed by the work we do — and the workplace can be a hostile environment for spirituality — we get sucked into idolatry. The worship of technology with its illusion of control is yet another avenue into idolatry.

Although the workplace is teeming with temptations to idolatry, it is also "the primary location for spiritual formation" (p. 127). When coupled with Sabbath-keeping, our workplace immersion in creation can keep us attuned to the God of creation, participating in his creative work.

Key Term

Sabbath: A weekly rhythm in which we stop our working and controlling in order to return worship and wonder — our attention to and adoration of God — to the center of our lives. Sabbath is the key protection against idolatry and turning other people into functions.

Quotations to Consider

"God worked in creation, which means that all our work is done in the context of God-work. Sabbath is a deliberate act of interference, an interruption of our work each week, a decree of no-work so that we are able to notice, to attend, to listen, to assimilate this comprehensive and majestic work of God, to orient our work in the work of God" (p. 110).

"Worship is the primary way in which the people of God stay in rhythm with the creation, find their place in creation, who they are and where they come from, internalizing the creation cadence of God . . ." (p. 114).

"Sabbath and work are integrated parts of an organic whole. Either apart from the other is crippled. . . . We cannot rightly understand Sabbath apart from work nor rightly understand work apart from Sabbath" (pp. 115, 116).

"There is more to work than work — there is God: God in completion, God in repose, God blessing, God making holy" (p. 116).

"We make idols in our workplaces when we reduce all relationships to functions that we can manage. We make idols in our workplaces when we reduce work to the dimensions of our egos and control" (p. 116).

"Sabbath is not primarily about us or how it benefits us; it is about God and how God forms us" (pp. 116-17).

"When we work we are most god-like, which means that it is in our work that it is easiest to develop god-pretensions" (p. 117).

"I don't see any way out of it: if we are going to live appropriately in the creation we must keep the Sabbath" (p. 117).

"All our ancestors agree that without silence and stillness there is no spirituality, no God-attentive, God-responsive life" (pp. 117-18).

"Fear-of-the-Lord is fear with the scary element deleted. And so it is often accompanied by the reassuring 'fear not.' The 'fear not' doesn't result in the absence of fear, but rather its transformation into 'fear-of-the-Lord.' But we still don't know what is going on. We still are not in control. We still are deep in mystery" (p. 121).

"I am not the center of my existence; I am not the sum-total of what matters; I don't know what will happen next" (p. 122).

"Without wonder the motivational energies for living well get dominated by anxiety and guilt" (p. 123).

"Along the way the primacy of God and his work in our lives gives way ever so slightly to the primacy of *our* work in God's kingdom, and we being thinking of ways that we can use God in what we are doing" (p. 124).

"We have become consumers of packaged spiritualities. This also is idolatry. We never think of using this term for it since everything we are buying or paying for is defined by the adjective 'Christian.' But idolatry it is nevertheless: God packaged as a product; God depersonalized and made available as a technique or program. The Christian market in idols has never been more brisk or lucrative" (p. 125).

Questions for Interaction

1. How much do you trust God to take care of your life? your family? your church? the world? Do you ever try to take over and then ask God to help you out?

2. In order to get our work right, we have to pay attention to God and his work. Sabbath gives us pause from our work just long enough to notice and attend to God and his work. Have you ever taken a walk along a route that you normally travel in a car? What did you notice on your walk that you'd never noticed as you sped by? How might the leisure of Sabbath-keeping similarly increase your God-awareness?

3. We are to do what is most loving. We keep Sabbath because we will never be slaves again or make anyone else a slave (Deut. 5:12-15). How is keeping the Sabbath for other people an act of love for them?

4. How does Sabbath-keeping protect our freedom? How does it promote social justice for others?

5. Refusing to wait and desiring Egyptian novelty led the Israelites to the Sinai idolatry. How do impatience and novelty impact your church worship?

6. "When we work we are most god-like, which means that it is in our work that it is easiest to develop god-pretensions" (p. 117). We're familiar with CEOs who seem to think of themselves as gods, but this warning actually includes all of us. In what ways are you god-like in your working?

7. "Cultivate solitude. Cultivate silence" (p. 118). Do you have stretches of time each week where you are silent, where you are alone? How do you protect and cultivate your quiet times?

8. "Without wonder the motivational energies for living well get dom-

inated by anxiety and guilt" (p. 123). How much of your church-related activity is motivated by anxiety and guilt?

Prayers

Psalm 92 is the one psalm specifically associated with the Sabbath. It begins in worship (verses 1-5), moves through considering the "enemies" (6-11), and ends with a hope so tangible that the future is rendered in the present tense (12-15). Read the psalm aloud and use the three movements to shape your time of praying together.

Christ Plays in History (1)

(pp. 131-47)

Summary

Welcome to the jungle.

Creation isn't the only context we find ourselves in. History spills out of creation. But not only does it spill out, it also spills all over creation. The wonder is marred with mess. ". . . everything is not so wonderful" (p. 133). In fact, the wonder of creation is easily obscured by the mess of history. "Much of life, much of *our* lives, consists in picking up the pieces of history, cleaning up the mess" (p. 133). Where creation presents us with life and more life, history presents us with death and more death. "Something is wrong here, dreadfully wrong" (p. 134).

The "school bullies" in their many forms — moral, physical, emotional, spiritual, political, economic — beat us up again and again. Tired of being beaten up in this flow of history, we are tempted to play by their rules, fighting back and becoming bullies ourselves. Bullies for Jesus.

Things are wrong, but our immersion in creation shouts, "This isn't how it was meant to be. You were created for something else." In other words, "Death provides the fundamental datum that something isn't working the way it was intended, accompanied by the feeling that we have every right to expect something other and better" (p. 137). Death flies in the face of the goodness of creation and calls for a response. The response is the death of Jesus.

Matching our disappointments with our own lives, is Jesus' life. "The life of Jesus is not a happy story, not a success story" (p. 137). No, it's a salvation story. "Jesus' death becomes the proclamation that our salvation is accomplished" (p. 138).

History is full of bulldozer-like people and forces. We tend either to be intimidated by them, running away and cloistering ourselves, or to exploit them, taking their methods as our own because of their effectiveness. But there's another way: the Jesus way. The way of Jesus is the way of suffering and death.

The suffering and death of Jesus is the ultimate proof that God's good creation has gone awry. And my own suffering and death are inevitable parts of my own history. But not only are they unavoidable, they're essential to salvation.

Jesus didn't hold history, with its suffering and death, at arm's length. He immersed himself in it. As much as we would like to avoid them at almost all costs, our paths as we follow Jesus go right through them, too. "The way Jesus did it becomes the way we do it" (p. 143).

The most common way to approach the mess of history is to turn up our nose and try to fix things through moralism. While morality is an aspect of creation — God has embedded right and wrong into his good creation — moralism is imposed on creation because of the mess of history. Moralism tries to fix the mess without God, saving ourselves on our own terms. Moralism calls for lots of things — except Jesus.

Key Terms

History: "The arena in which God carries out his work of salvation" (p. 138). It's less a detailed, factual accounting of the precise events of the past than it is the narrative of "actual people and circumstances in their dealings with God, and in God's dealings with them" (p. 138).

Morality: The basic structure of right and wrong that is embedded into creation. The basic, God-given goodness of creation.

Moralism: The attempt to circumvent the need for salvation by imposing a system in which we don't do anything wrong and don't need to be saved. It is an attempt at goodness without God.

Quotations to Consider

"History is lubricated by tears. Prayer, maybe most prayer (two thirds of the psalms are laments), is accompanied by tears. All these tears are gathered up and absorbed in the tears of Jesus" (p. 138).

"God was alive, always and everywhere working his will, challenging people with his call, evoking faith and obedience, calling them into a worshiping community, showing his love and compassion, and working out judgments on sin. And none of this 'in general' or 'at large,' but at particular times, in specific places, with named persons: history" (p. 139).

"History is the medium in which God works salvation. . . . We cannot get closer to God by distancing ourselves from the mess of history" (p. 139).

"If we want anything to do with God as biblically revealed there is no escaping history" (p. 140).

"God is equally present and active in the history recorded in the Scriptures and the history recorded in our contemporary textbooks" (p. 140).

"God, it turns out, does not require good people in order to do good work. As one medieval saying has it, 'God draws straight lines with a crooked stick.' He can and does work with us, whatever the moral and spiritual condition in which he finds us. God, we realize, does some of his best work using the most unlikely people" (pp. 140-41).

"Suffering and death, the worst that life can hand us, is the very stuff out of which salvation is fashioned" (p. 143).

"The most common way that we in the Christian community have of avoiding or marginalizing Jesus' death is by constructing a way of life that is safe and secure and guilt-free" (p. 144).

"Morality is built into reality as deeply and inescapably as atoms and protons and neutrons. We are moral beings to the core — the very universe is moral. Right and wrong are embedded in the creation. It matters what is done, said, believed, even thought. Morality is fundamental and nonnegotiable" (p. 145).

"Moralism means constructing a way of life in which I have no need of a saving God. Moralism is dead; morality is alive" (p. 145).

"Moralism works from strength, not weakness. Moralism uses God (or the revelation of God) in order not to need God any longer. Moral codes are used as stepping stones to independence from God" (p. 145).

"Procrustes and his bed are the stuff of moralism: a strategy carried out by people who are contemptuous of our particularities and force us to fit a preconceived pattern" (p. 146).

Questions for Interaction

1. All the names and places in Scripture show God's tie to history. Read a list from Scripture (possible passages include anything from 1 Chronicles 1–9, Nehemiah 7, Numbers 1–3, and Matthew 1). Do you find such passages boring or interesting? How might they enlarge your view of what God has done and is doing in the world? How would the passages be different if your group members were listed? We tend to try to fit God into our history instead of trying to fit into God's history. How might such lists restore a biblical perspective on our named place in God's history? How might these lists of ancient names shape the way you pray?

2. Who is/are your "Garrison Johns," your "school bullies"? Who taught you through painful interactions that all is not right with the world (and by extension with your life)? What events taught you this? (Be prepared to stop and pray for anyone whose "Garrison Johns" wounds are still causing significant pain.)

3. People are always tempted to separate God from history, coming up with "pure" theologies, which are nice ideas about God, but don't actually reflect the God of history, the God whose story is revealed in Scripture. Referring to God as faithful or just or compassionate means nothing without the telling of stories in which God has shown himself to be faithful or just or compassionate. Take some time to tie your theology to your personal history, sharing a God story with the group.

4. Scripture is less of a tool to use than a story to live into. Who is in control if Scripture is used as a tool, God or us? (What do you do with your tools when you're not using them?) Who is in control if Scripture is a story that is entered into, the Author or the character?

5. Eugene Peterson writes of "boutique spirituality" in which we use "God as decoration, God as enhancement." Discuss the difference between a life in which God is an ornament or a tool for self-fulfillment and a life in which God and his story give the shape and substance.

6. Discuss the difference between morality and moralism. Why is it important to distinguish between the two, retaining morality while rejecting moralism? In what ways have you slid from morality and into moralism in the past?

7. The story of Procrustes' bed is gruesome but enlightening. Have you ever been in a group (Christian or otherwise) that was Procrustean in approach, trying to make you fit its image of the way you ought to be? What sort of things did they try to lop off? What sort of things did they try to stretch?

Prayers

History is the venue of both sin and salvation. Use the prayer of poet John Donne (1572-1631) to shape your praying about both sin and salvation.

"O eternal God . . . let me, in spite of me, be of so much use to your glory, that by your mercy to my sin, other sinners may see how much sin you can pardon."

Christ Plays in History (2)

(pp. 147-81)

Summary

"Salvation" is the word that brings together everything Jesus is doing in history. "Salvation is the name of this game that is history" (p. 148).

"Jesus saves" has been turned into bumper stickers and slogans, thinning it out and turning it into a one-shot deal. To regain its broad scope as the story of history, we turn to the book of Exodus.

Exodus begins at the low point of Israel's history — a historical dead-end. Mighty, magnificent Egypt absolutely dominated them in many ways. But the biblical writers actually ignored the marvels of Egypt. They were interested in God.

Because of this God-focus, two midwives defy the powerful Pharaoh's command to kill all the baby boys. Life emerges from death. "World leaders are minor players in the biblical way of writing and participating in history" (p. 151). The ordinary, outsider, ill-equipped people of God (from Shiphrah and Puah to Moses and me) are the decisive players in salvation history.

Much of what we experience is of the absence of God, not feelings of his presence. The psalmists teach us how to pray about this feeling of abandonment. And yet God, who revealed himself by the name I AM THAT I AM is "present to us and personal with us" (p. 158). Whatever our feelings say, God is here.

The conditions we live in impress us and are impressed into us. Oppressors almost always seem like they're the only game going, while God seems to be gone. So, we fall for life on the oppressors' terms, not God's terms. The Hebrews had been shaped by Egyptian domination and death. They needed an "exorcism" of sorts. They needed a whole new way of thinking and believing to get out from under that dominion. The same is true for us in our culture.

What people often refer to as the "real world" is truly not the real world, but a defaced form of it. Our imaginations need scrubbing so we can clearly see the real world of God. The ten plagues demonstrated that the so-called real world of Pharaoh's Egypt wasn't Reality. God was the true Reality, the true sovereign. Knowing God was the goal of the plagues.

Likewise, Jesus' cleansing of the temple was a purging of the imagination and a sovereignty issue. He is the authority and the way to know God.

We cloud our imaginations with our own desires and miss out on the salvation going on around us. Those frustrated desires lead to anger.

One of our desires is to reduce salvation to ourselves. But salvation is less an individual assent to some ideas about God than a participation as a community in the story of God. We tend to focus on how important we are, when salvation is something God does while we watch and wait.

To remember that salvation is God's thing that we get in on, the Jews celebrated Passover by retelling the story, eating the meal, and singing the song.

Worship is the most appropriate response to salvation. Singing gathers together all that cannot be expressed in normal words. Worship draws all of life into the lens of salvation.

History is defined by what God does to save, not by what we do to mess things up. The newspaper is the epitome of sin-defined history, but worship restores our God-defined perspective. We tend to reduce worship to an hour or so a week when worship is what takes our reduced lives and expands them into the big world of God.

Spiritualizing salvation reduces it to how we as individuals feel at the moment. It is, therefore, essential to keep salvation rooted in historical reality. If we lack deep historical roots, the evil around us causes us to either live timidly (in fear of it) or obnoxiously (barking against it). But the God who saved is the God who saves. We don't fear history or dismiss it, we look for God's actions in it.

Quotations to Consider

"'Salvation' is the single word that most succinctly characterizes this play of Jesus in history" (p. 147).

"Salvation is God's work: *Jesus* saves. Incompetence may be the essential qualification, lest we impatiently and presumptuously take over the business and start managing a vast and intricate economy that we have no way of comprehending" (p. 152).

"The story in which God does his saving work arises among a people whose primary experience of God is his absence. . . . Where was God all this time?" (p. 153).

"Belief in God does not exempt us from feelings of abandonment by God" (p. 154).

"Any understanding of God that doesn't take into account God's silence is a half truth — in effect, a cruel distortion — and leaves us vulnerable to manipulation and exploitation by leaders who are quite willing to fill in the biblical blanks with what the Holy Spirit never tells us" (p. 156).

"Salvation is a far larger country than creation" (p. 167).

"This is a major and never-ending task, this exorcism of the culture's lies and pretensions from the Christian imagination so that God's sovereignty in history can be received in a life large with salvation" (p. 169).

"God is the subject, people are the object. God does it, we get in on it" (p. 172).

"Song is heightened speech. . . . Song does not explain, it expresses. . . . Song is more than words and there are no words to convey what that 'more' is precisely. Song is one of the two ways (silence is the other) of giving witness to the transcendent" (p. 176).

Questions for Interaction

1. Those who know themselves to be saved by God always burst forth in song. What "songs, hymns, and spiritual songs" express the most for you?

2. After all of the talk of suffering and death in history, Eugene Peterson returns us to Christ "playing" in salvation. How does the word "play" strike you as a description of this serious business of salvation? How does it respond to the bumper sticker slogans that have reduced salvation to a cliché?

3. "Incompetence may be the essential qualification" for our participation in God's salvation work, because it keeps us humble and out of the way. What's an area of weakness in you that God has used to help others?

4. Moses isn't to be a model to copy but a companion to walk alongside of. How does turning biblical characters into models or heroes ruin them? How does approaching them as companions restore their usefulness to us?

5. The salvation story has long silences, long periods of inactivity, long absences of God. Have you felt the silence, inactivity, and absence of God? Is it a part of your current experience? How does it help to know that this is a common experience? Should you judge the state of your spirituality by how close you feel to God? Do you?

6. The Psalms have been the prayer book for God's people for centuries. The psalmists give us "license to pray our complaints about the way this whole salvation business is being conducted" (p. 154). Do you feel comfortable complaining to God about the way he does things? How do the Psalms give voice to the way you feel about God?

7. Discuss the role of story, meal, and song in entering into salvation. How does your church enlarge its salvation imagination through the telling of the story, the eating of the meal, and the singing of songs?

8. Eugene Peterson writes, ". . . if we can do it or at least manage it, it is no longer salvation" (p. 177). What's the difference between self-help and salvation?

9. Sin is real and we have to face it. But we are more determined by God's salvation, not by our sin. How seriously do you take your sin? How seriously do you take God's salvation?

10. Spiritualizing salvation reduces it to a feeling. How does re-rooting salvation in historical reality give it more substance?

Prayers

The Egyptian plagues and the cleansing of the temple are exorcisms of sorts, cleansing the imagination. Use the following prayer to cleanse your praying imagination:

> In this world of sports stars and superstars, you alone are God.
> In this world of stalkers and stock markets, you alone are God.
> In this world of presidents and prime ministers, you alone are God.
> In this world of shopping malls and sale prices, you alone are God.
> In this world of terrorists and armed forces, you alone are God.
> In this world of cell phones and software upgrades, you alone
>   are God.
> In this world of salaries and lay-offs, you alone are God.
> In this world of diets and lattes, you alone are God.
> In this world of money, sex, and power, you alone are God.

Christ Plays in History (3)

(pp. 181-99)

Summary

The Bible as a whole is a story. That form is important and not accidental. We need to retain the Bible's storied nature. Stories are bigger than we are, enabling us to respond in ways that are bigger than we are — we're expanded by them. They are, by nature, invitational. They call us in, inviting our participation in them. But if we insist on being in control, we have to reduce the story to manageable concepts and programs, which is to reduce ourselves in the process.

Stories pull us in so that we're more than spectators. And while moral, stories can't be reduced to moralisms.

Salvation is not something any of us can control. At the same time, it's not just something that happens to us while we passively sit by. We are drawn in as participants with the freedom of knowing that it doesn't all depend on us. It's not that we're irresponsible; it's that God is responsible.

There are pedestals for no one except for Jesus (and his is a cross). Mark makes sure that as impressive as the apostles may have been to the early Christian community, they are never allowed to eclipse Jesus. The Gospel is never about them, although they are included. It's always about Jesus. The way "Stumpfinger" Mark (p. 184) wrote his Gospel makes sure that our attention is never diverted from Jesus.

The last half of St. Mark's Gospel is dominated by death talk. The more relaxed pace of the first half is replaced by the urgency and gravity of the goal of crucifixion. No other part of Jesus' life is told with as much detail as that given to his death. ". . . the plot and emphasis and meaning of Jesus is his death" (p. 187).

Jesus' death is defined by the words "voluntary" and "sacrificial." It was not an accident and it was meant "as a means to life for others" (p. 188). Even so, its final definition is in terms of resurrection. It is therefore neither tragic, nor procrastinated.

Eugene Peterson points out the detailed, chiastic structure of the story of Jesus' death in Mark's Gospel. This immerses us in the story in order to show us the completeness of what Jesus did as he died for our salvation.

At the middle of Mark's Gospel are two stories which, side-by-side, give us God's No and God's Yes. In the first, Peter tries to avoid the cross. In the second, he tries to grab the glory. He got it wrong and we've been getting it wrong ever since.

We are invited to participate. Not to take over.

Key Terms

Gospel: The mature completion of centuries of Hebrew storytelling and the clear revelation of God in Jesus told "in a way that invites, more, *insists* on, our participation" (p. 182). In other words, Gospel reveals God and engages us.

Myth: A made-up story told to make a moral lesson "which more or less turns us into spectators of the supernatural" (p. 182).

Colobodactylus: A nickname for Mark, the traditional author of the Gospel bearing his name. A Latin word meaning "stumpfinger."

Chiasm, chiastic: The Greek letter *chi* is X-shaped. A chiasm is a literary form of repeating similar material in a way that makes an X shape. For instance, if A = Frank and B = dog, the following sentence would be chiastic, following an A B B A pattern: Frank bought a dog and the dog lives with Frank. Most Western literature generally uses parallelism, following an A B A B pattern. But Hebrew and Greek literature generally used a chiastic pattern. In more complex chiasms, like the one pointed out in pages 189-94, the emphasis is always on the center. It can be thought of as a pyramid: Each step up brings you closer to the point and each step down the other side moves outward from the point.

Quotations to Consider

"Stories invite us into a world other than ourselves, and, if they are good and true stories, a world larger than ourselves" (pp. 181-82).

". . . the minute we abandon the story, we reduce reality to the dimensions of our minds and feelings and experience" (p. 182).

"We don't figure Jesus out, we don't search Jesus out, we don't get Jesus on our terms. Jesus and the salvation that he embodied are not consumer items" (p. 183).

"Mark was not a journalist. . . . Nor was he a propagandist. . . . His Gospel is spiritual theology in action, a form of writing that draws us into a living participation with the text" (p. 195).

"There is always a strong ascetic element in salvation. Following Jesus means *not* following the death-procrastinating, death-denying practices of a culture that by obsessively pursuing life under the aegis of idols and ideologies ends up with a life that is so constricted and diminished that it is hardly worthy of the name" (p. 196).

"The art of saying 'no' sets us free to follow Jesus" (p. 196).

"Our senses have been dulled by sin. The world, for all its vaunted celebration of sensuality, is relentlessly anaesthetic. . . . Our senses require healing and rehabilitation so that they are adequate for receiving and responding to visitations and appearances of Spirit, God's Holy Spirit . . ." (p. 197).

"We are not simply *told* that Jesus is the Son of God; we not only *become* beneficiaries of his atonement; we are invited to die his death and live his life with the freedom and dignity of participants" (p. 199).

Questions for Interaction

1. Why is Scripture mostly story? How do stories draw us in in ways that non-fiction can't? What are some stories that continue to draw you in and shape your life?
2. "Jesus provides both the context and content for salvation." What does that leave for us?
3. Peter was the lead apostle and a huge figure in the early Church. Why does Mark practically write "Peter out of the story by making it clear that Peter is, in actual fact, the lead sinner" (p. 185)? Do you ever feel "written out" of your own life story?
4. "The death of Jesus is not tragic" (p. 188). What deaths do you know of or have you witnessed that were tragic? How were those deaths different from Jesus' horrible yet not tragic death?
5. "The death of Jesus is not procrastinated" (p. 188). What do you think and feel about modern medicine's ability to delay death? What's right with it? What's wrong with it? How are these procrastinated deaths different from Jesus' death?
6. Eugene Peterson gives a sketch of the story of Jesus' death. What did you learn that was new to you? How helpful was it to see the chiastic pattern of the story?
7. Peter tried to avoid the cross and grab the glory. Sounds like a beer ad! How does this mimic the world? In what ways have you found yourself following suit?

Prayers

A variety of services have historically been held on Good Friday. In one, seven candles are lit and as each of the seven sayings of Jesus from the cross are read, one of the candles is snuffed out. Consider either a full service or simply using the seven sayings from the cross to guide your time of prayer.

"And about three o'clock Jesus cried with a loud voice, 'Eli, Eli, lema sabachthani?' that is, 'My God, my God, why have you forsaken me?'" (Matt. 27:46).

"Then Jesus said, 'Father, forgive them; for they do not know what they are doing.' And they cast lots to divide his clothing" (Luke 23:34).

"He replied, 'Truly I tell you, today you will be with me in Paradise'" (Luke 23:43).

"Then Jesus, crying with a loud voice, said, 'Father, into your hands I commend my spirit.' Having said this, he breathed his last" (Luke 23:46).

"When Jesus saw his mother and the disciple whom he loved standing beside her, he said to his mother, 'Woman, here is your son.' Then he said to the disciple, 'Here is your mother.' And from that hour the disciple took her into his own home" (John 19:26-27).

"After this, when Jesus knew that all was now finished, he said (in order to fulfill the scripture), 'I am thirsty'" (John 19:28).

"When Jesus had received the wine, he said, 'It is finished.' Then he bowed his head and gave up his spirit" (John 19:30).

Christ Plays in History (4)

(pp. 200-222)

If your group has not been eating meals together up to this point, start with this session. If they have, ask, "How has eating meals together shaped our time together and the rest of the week?" Try fixing a meal together instead of eating potluck.

If your church polity allows it, share Communion together as part of the session.

Summary

Communion — however we do it and whatever we call it — is the focal practice, the fear-of-the-Lord practice, the thing we do as participants in salvation. "Remember and proclaim are the magnetic poles of the Eucharist" (p. 201).

Without Eucharist, we tend to reduce Jesus to an Example to imitate, a Teacher to learn from, or a Hero to be inspired by. And although he is a great example, teacher, and hero and there is a lot to imitate, learn, and be inspired by, the Eucharist reminds us that salvation is about receiving forgiveness from sins.

The way of the world in dealing with what's wrong with the world is by means of force, education, entertainment, and economic improvement. Those all have their place, but none deals with the real problem: sin.

Instead of dealing with what's wrong with the world through force, by education, by entertainment, or by economic improvement, Jesus deals with it by sacrifice. And the sacrifice he offers is himself. Jesus takes the problem into himself and "becomes the sacrifice that is transformed into the life of salvation" (p. 204).

In establishing the Eucharist, Jesus created a ritual. At their best, rituals preserve mystery, speak of a reality larger than ourselves, and protect certain relationships. They preserve meaningful things from being tinkered with.

Four basic actions give shape to the liturgy of Communion: Take, bless, break, give. We offer and Jesus takes from us. We offer to Jesus and he offers it to the Father. What we bring, who we are must be broken. Not only are our offerings broken and us with them, but Jesus himself is broken. And finally, Jesus gives us back what we gave to him, but it is no longer what we brought.

The Lord's Supper spills over into a lifetime of suppers. A life of shared meals and hospitality is the expression of a saved life. Since hospitality is central to our understanding of God and salvation — we are invited into the "home" life of God — it also becomes central to our understanding of ourselves and of evangelism — we invite others into our homes and hearts.

In a technologized world, where efficiency and speed are king and queen, table meals of hospitality slow us down, restoring the leisure that relationships require.

God saves in no other way than sacrifice. That doesn't just mean Jesus; it also means us. And living this saved life of hospitality means sacrifice as well. We don't just do it on our own terms. It is sacrifice for the sake of others. Discomfort is an unavoidable ingredient.

Key Terms

Remember: Reorienting ourselves to what Christ did.

Proclaim: Taking what Christ did to the world.

Quotations to Consider

"Before *we do* anything for God, we receive what God in *Christ does* for us" (p. 200).

"The Supper is a preached parable" (p. 201).

"Remember and proclaim are the magnetic poles of the Eucharist" (p. 201).

"Receiving the Eucharist, like other aspects of the fear-of-the-Lord, is rooted deep in the soil of not-doing. In this intentional, disciplined passivity we become aware that the work of salvation is far wider and deeper than just us" (p. 202).

"Sacrifice is at the center of the work of salvation. Sacrifice is God's way of dealing with what is wrong in history. . . . It is God's way of dealing with sin" (p. 203).

"These offerings are our best but they are also an acknowledgment that our best is not good enough. Se we place our best on the altar and see what God can do with it, to see if he can do any better with it than we have been able to do. We let go of our best, give it up. So what happens next?" (p. 204).

"God has used the stuff of our sins to save us from our sins" (p. 204).

"I cannot take charge of a ritual, I can only enter in — or not. Neither can I engage in a ritual by myself; others are involved" (p. 206).

"[Jesus] refuses nothing of who we are, what we have done" (p. 208).

"God receives us and what we bring to him, just as we are. God does not extort; God does not exploit us; God does not force us. He takes only what we offer. 'Coercion is no attribute of God'" (p. 208).

"Jesus is both the sacrifice and the priest who offers the sacrifice. . . . This is the act that centers and defines all of history" (p. 209).

"But the Jesus who saves us needs access to what is within us and so exposes our insides, our inadequacies, our 'cover-ups.' At the Table we are not permitted to be self-enclosed. We are not permitted to be self-sufficient. The breaking of our pride and self-approval is not a bad thing;

it opens us to new life, to saving action. We come crusted over, hardened into ourselves. We soon discover that God is working deep within us, beneath our surface lies and poses, to bring new life. We cannot remain self-enclosed on this altar . . ." (p. 210).

"Jesus could not have been more clear about it: this abundant life, this ransomed life, this salvation life is a life of communion, of intimate relationship of sacrificial love in and with the Father, Son, and Holy Ghost" (p. 211).

"Any understanding of salvation that separates us from others is false and sooner or later cripples our participation in what God in Christ is doing in history, saving the world" (p. 211).

"It is striking how much of Jesus' life is told in settings defined by meals" (p. 212).

"Daily meals with family, friends, and guests, acts of hospitality every one, are the most natural and frequent settings for working out the personal and social implications of the gospel" (p. 214).

". . . a primary, maybe *the* primary, venue for evangelism in Jesus' life was the meal" (p. 215).

"A life of hospitality keeps us in intimate touch with our families and the traditions in which we are reared, personally available to friends and guests, morally related to the hungry and homeless, and, perhaps most important of all, participants in the context and conditions in which Jesus lived his life, using the language he used for the salvation of the world" (p. 216).

"A meal engages personal participation at the most basic level of our lives. It is virtually impossible to be detached and uninvolved when we are sharing a meal with someone" (p. 217).

Annie Dillard . . . [said]: "a life without sacrifice is an abomination" (p. 219).

"Hospitality is daily practice in keeping sacrifice local and immediate . . ." (219).

". . . we take the kitchen to be as essential in the work of salvation as is the sanctuary" (p. 220).

"We are not self-sufficient. We live by life and the lives given to and for us" (p. 222).

Questions for Interaction

1. However we do it and whatever we call it, almost all Christians practice Communion. How often does your church celebrate the Lord's Supper? What elements make up your practice? If you've had Communion in other churches, what is different about their practice? What is the same?

2. We have offerings instead of sacrifices, giving money instead of stuff. How does this change the way we think about our giving? Do you ever designate your giving, trying to control your "gift"? Do you ever give "stuff" instead of (or as well as) money? How does that change the nature of your giving?

3. The Lord's Supper is a ritual created by Jesus. Do you experience rituals as something dead and meaningless? Or do you experience ritual as alive with all sorts of meaning that couldn't be conveyed otherwise? What kills ritual? What makes ritual alive?

4. Many Christian traditions focus on a "sinner's prayer" as the means of salvation. How does this turn salvation into a "private deal with God"? How does this undermine the communal nature of the salvation life?

5. Eugene Peterson links hospitality and evangelism. Have you linked the two before? How can hospitality be reduced by attempts to evangelize? How can real hospitality lead to real evangelism?

6. Eugene Peterson asks, "By marginalizing meals of hospitality in our daily lives have we inadvertently diminished the work of evangelism? And is there anything to be done about it?" (p. 215).

7. Do you read or watch TV when you eat? How does reading or watching TV when eating keep you from "tasting" both food and relationship?

8. We've been eating meals our whole lives and not noting the Eucharistic elements. How can we eat meals in a way that makes us more alive to God and to each other?

Prayers

The following Eucharist prayer is from the third century non-canonical book The Apocryphal Acts of Thomas. It immerses us in the sacrament as it prays through the passion of Christ. Use it as an entry point in praying and receiving Communion yourself.

> May this your sacrament, Lord Jesus Christ,
> bring life to us and pardon for our sins,
> to us for whom you suffered your passion.
>
> For our sake you drank gall
> to kill in us the bitterness
> that is the Enemy's.
>
> For our sake you drank sour wine
> to strengthen what is weak in us.
>
> For our sake you were spat upon
> to bathe us in the dew of immortality.
>
> You were struck with a frail reed
> to strengthen what is frail in us
> and give us life for all eternity.
>
> You were crowned with thorns
> to crown those who believe in you
> with that ever-green garland, your charity.
>
> You were wrapped in a shroud
> to clothe us in your all-enfolding strength.
>
> You were laid in a new grave
> to give us new grace in all ages likewise new.

Christ Plays in Community (1)

(pp. 223-44)

Summary

We are not to be tourists in this world of creation and salvation. We were made to be participants, and we love participating. Our problem is all these other people that we're lumped with. They're messy and we don't necessarily like them all.

Ironically, the very people who are invited to participate in God's creating and saving yawn through worship. Why? We have no concept of holiness — God's or our own.

As with creation and salvation, we're not in charge of sanctification — the making of holiness. "We don't begin a holy life by wanting a holy life. . . . Living a holy life, the Christian equivalent of revolution, begins with Jesus' resurrection" (p. 230).

This resurrection community that we enter is neither of our making or choosing.

What we're after is "living the Jesus life in the Jesus way" (p. 234). To prepare us for this, Jesus prays for us and gives us his Spirit. Before he sends the Spirit, he himself leaves. But when he's gone, it is the Spirit who makes our lives and work continuous with Jesus' life and work.

We tend to think of sects as splinter groups that have strange beliefs about God. But any special interest group that willfully separates from the larger community is guilty of sectarianism. And if one of the primary purposes of the Holy Spirit is the creation of Christian community, then breaking apart that community is an offense to God. Sectarianism is a lived heresy.

Sects are always appealing because they appeal to that part of us that is hungry for attention, the insatiable ego. Narcissus is their icon. Self is their diet. Everything is prefixed with self. But Jesus is moving us from self to community. His great prayer for us is that we be one.

When we reduce church to a style of music, a form of liturgy, a pastor's charisma, or a set of programs, we've moved from church as a community that we enter to a set of "services" that we gather around ourselves in order to feed ourselves. The purpose of church becomes the worship of Me.

Key Terms

Kerygma: proclamation of what Christ has done for us that we take part in but don't make ourselves.

Spiritual formation: "primarily what the Spirit does, forming the resurrection life of Christ in us" (p. 237).

Sectarianism: "deliberately and willfully leaving the large community . . . embarking on a path of special interests with some others, whether few or many, who share similar tastes and concerns" (pp. 239-40). A heresy of community; a blasphemy of the Spirit's community-building.

Selfism: "the conceit that I don't need others as they are but only for what they can do for me. Selfism reduces life to my appetites and needs and preferences" (p. 241).

Quotations to Consider

"We are not tourists here . . ." (p. 225).

". . . there can be no maturity in the spiritual life, no obedience in following Jesus, no wholeness in the Christian life apart from an immersion and embrace of community. I am not myself by myself" (p. 226).

"People can think correctly and behave rightly and worship politely and still live badly — live anemically, live individualistically self-enclosed lives, live bored and insipid and trivial lives" (p. 229).

"Jesus did not raise himself; he was raised. And we do not raise ourselves; we are raised" (p. 231).

". . . resurrection is primarily a matter of living in a wondrous creation, embracing a salvation history, and then taking our place in a holy community: *receive the Holy Spirit*" (p. 231).

". . . we are in community whether we like it or not. We do not choose to be in this community; by virtue of the resurrection of Jesus, this is the company we keep" (p. 231).

"The leaving and sending work together, back and forth, back and forth. Jesus' absence from them becomes the Spirit's presence in them. Everything Jesus said and did among them is to be continued in what they (we!) say and do" (p. 236).

"Sectarianism is to the community what heresy is to theology, a willful removal of a part from the whole" (p. 240).

"Sects are composed of men and women who reinforce their basic selfism by banding together with others who are pursuing similar brands of selfism . . ." (p. 242).

"But holy living, resurrection living, is not a self-project. We are a *people* of God and cannot live holy lives, resurrection lives, as individuals. We are not a self-defined community; we are a God-defined community" (p. 244).

"A sect is a front for narcissism. . . . This is just a cover for our individualism: we reduce the community to the conditions congenial to the imperial self" (p. 244).

"Sects are termites in the Father's house" (p. 244).

Questions for Interaction

1. The Holy Spirit makes our lives and work continuous with Jesus' life and work. Do you have a sense that your life and work are con-

tinuous with that of Jesus? Or does that sound too big and bold to be true? Discuss.

2. God sent his Spirit and we wait to receive the Spirit. There's a lot of waiting involved. In what areas are you feeling impatient with God?

3. How does the resurrection of Jesus affect the way you think about and live your life from day to day? Does it have any effect?

4. What do you think it means for the church to be the "resurrection community"?

5. What is the difference between a church and a special interest group?

6. Have you ever been "church shopping"? What's odd about that phrase? What was it that caused you to stop and settle down with the quirky people of your church?

7. People leave churches for a whole variety of reasons, almost all of which have to do with "I don't like this" or "That's not meeting my needs." Have you ever been one of these? (Don't worry, you're among forgiving friends.) Have you watched anyone leave your church community recently for similar reasons? How did these departures make you feel?

8. List the reasons why people leave churches or even start new ones — for example, music, programs, theology, ethnicity, sermons, pastor, interpersonal, and so on. Discuss each one. How much is legitimate and how much is just well-disguised narcissism?

9. Have you ever been a part of a church that split? What were the stated reasons? What do you think were the real reasons?

Prayers

The following prayer is by William Laud (1573-1645), Archbishop of Canterbury. Consider using it as a guide for your praying for your church community and the Church universal. Notice that he relies on God to take care of the church in every way.

"Most gracious Father, we humbly beg you for your Holy Catholic Church; that you would be pleased to fill it with all truth, in all peace. Where it is corrupt, purify it; where it is in error, direct it; where in anything it is amiss, reform it. Where it is right, strengthen and confirm it; where it is in want, provide for it; where it is divided and rent asunder, do make up for the breaches in it, O holy one of Israel."

Christ Plays in Community (2)

(pp. 245-66)

Summary

The book of Deuteronomy provides our first grounding text for community.

When the southern kingdom of Judah came under the reign of the child-king Josiah, it had suffered years of moral, political, and spiritual mess. The more exciting gods of the dominant Assyrian culture had been important and consumed with abandon. But when Josiah was 26, the book of the Law was found: Deuteronomy. And when it was read aloud, the nation changed. Josiah reformed the people of God as a community of worship and love.

Deuteronomy is a sermon: It's God's words to God's people. It doesn't say anything new. It brings what was said before and makes it a living reality here and now.

Getting saved is easy — God does it and there we are, saved. But becoming community . . . that's another story. The greatest obstacle to the Christian life and community is grumbling, as people focus on their wish-dreams instead of being the community God has made them to be. But the Ten Words, the Ten Commandments, help, making community at least possible.

The Shema (Deut. 6:4) is the creed of Israel. It binds belief to love. Love becomes the most characteristic word to describe not just our relationship with God, but with one another. Together, the Ten Words and the Shema provide the framework within which real community can exist. "The Ten Words set down the conditions for living in community. The creed provides the unifying focus (God only) and integrating motive (love)" (p. 263).

Quotations to Consider

"A sermon changes words about God into words from God" (p. 249).

"Even when a sermon is clumsy or inept, when it keeps the language of the community local and personal it has its use" (p. 249).

"The three adjectives — free, loving, just — are basic to community" (p. 252).

"Here are five God-conditions apart from which you can never have community. Ponder. Realize. Imagine. Embrace. Worship" (p. 253).

"Here are five human-conditions that cannot be violated if you are going to live in community, no matter what you feel or think. Name. Respect. Listen. Honor. Serve" (p. 253).

". . . if we want to live in community, this is the first condition: God without rivals, God without secretly holding on to other options" (p. 254).

"[Idols] are gods with all the God taken out so that we can continue to be our own gods" (p. 254).

"When we reduce God to a name among other names, all names eventually become depersonalized" (p. 255).

"Community cannot flourish without a sabbath" (p. 256).

"I am who I am only in a relation of honor and reverence to others — and the first and most enduring relation to others that we are aware of is to mother and father" (p. 257).

"We do not simplify our lives by getting rid of other lives . . ." (p. 258).

"Sexual desire is not allowed a life of its own. Sexuality is a community, not a private affair" (p. 258).

"Language is the community's lifeblood . . ." (p. 258).

"To covet is to fantasize a life other than what is given to me" (p. 259).

". . . there are simply no private actions — everything is personal but nothing is private. Everything we do is connected with everything else" (p. 259).

"Israel's creed is not bare dogma regarding God; it is witness. As we recite it we also become witnesses" (p. 260).

". . . if love does not shape the way we speak and act, we falsify the creed, we confess a lie. Believing without loving is what gives religion a bad name. Believing without loving destroys lives" (p. 261).

". . . conditions of sin and death are unavoidably inherent in community in general, but in the people of God community in particular" (p. 264).

". . . we who want to get in on what God does in the way God does it in all matters of community, will have to give up pretensions of shaping an organization that the world will think is wonderful as we parade our accomplishments to the tune of 'worship' or 'evangelism'" (p. 266).

Questions for Interaction

1. If you go to church, you hear sermons, whether you like them or not. What's the purpose of a sermon?
2. Being saved doesn't necessarily lead to community. What conflicts currently exist in your church? Take some time to pray about them.
3. What would your ideal church look like? What does your church look like now? Where are the gaps? What will it take for you to get over them?
4. Eugene Peterson names three adjectives — free, loving, just — that he considers basic to community. What would happen to a community that wasn't free? Wasn't loving? Wasn't just?
5. Why does Eugene Peterson call the following terms the five "God-conditions" without which community cannot exist — ponder, realize, imagine, embrace, worship?
6. Read the Ten Words from Deuteronomy 5:6-21 and then consider the following questions based on each of them:
   a. Why is God the essential context for community?

b. Why is it so tempting to have a god without dealing with God, a something to control instead of a Someone to love?

c. Has anyone butchered or forgotten your name recently? Why are names so important?

d. Why don't people keep Sabbath? "Is it because we don't like letting go of the controls? Is it because we want to be important and if we aren't observed doing something in the community we won't be noticed? Is it because if we let down our guard someone will take advantage of us or take over our position?" (p. 256).

e. What is the correlation between how you treat your parents and how you treat God?

f. Do you ever have the feeling that simply cutting someone out of your life would make your life more agreeable? Why won't this work?

g. "Sexuality is a community, not a private affair" (p. 258). Do you agree or disagree? How does this shape our approach to sex and marriage?

h. "Things are sacred and inviolable" (p. 258). How does the sacredness of things change the way you deal with them?

i. How does lying kill the words we speak? Whose word do you trust? Whose do you distrust? Why?

j. Admitting what we covet takes the power out it. What do you covet?

7. Think of ways that you (and the church in a culture that encourages it) have privatized not just your possessions and politics and finances and sexuality, but your faith. How are the Ten Words weakened when they are "individualized as a code for personal morality"? How would restoring their communal nature strengthen the community and our own personal practice of them?

8. How does a creed-supported love for God keep human love from atrophying to whim and fancy?

9. Moses' song is an Amazing Grace, singing our sin and God's faithfulness. Do we sing any other songs like Moses' song? How do the songs we sing in worship shape us (or not) as a holy community?

10. No amount of great teaching and preaching, no amount of revelation will keep the community of God from falling into sin. Take time to repent not of your individual sins, but of your demand that the Christian community conform to your wishes for perfection.

Prayers

Use the *Shema*, the creed of Israel, to give shape to your praying. Oneness. Love. Heart/mind. Soul. Strength.

"Hear, O Israel: The Lord is our God, the Lord alone. You shall love the Lord your God with all your heart, and with all your soul, and with all your might" (Deut. 6:4-5).

SESSION 13

Christ Plays in Community (3)

(pp. 267-99)

Summary

The grounding text of Luke/Acts ties the Jesus story of Luke with the Jesus-community story of Acts. Although our Bibles don't present them side-by-side, they are a seamless whole.

Luke presents the conception of Jesus as impossible, an act of the Holy Spirit alone. But the birth of Jesus is completely natural. Likewise, although conceived supernaturally by the Spirit, the Christian community lives a life common to all humanity.

The Holy Spirit acts powerfully and empowers the community. But it's not the impersonal power of tyrant or technology, it's the personal power of community-creating holy love.

The Holy Spirit is God present to us. Prayer is us present to God. Prayer pulls us into the Holy Spirit's presence, God's way of working through and speaking to us. Luke's telling of the birth story teaches us five ways to pray. (1) Our prayers join God's "praying" — God's conversation with us (the *Fiat mihi*). (2) Our prayers join us in the whole scope of what God has done, is doing, and will do (the *Magnificat*). (3) Our prayers join those of the saints before us (the *Benedictus*). (4) Our prayers are joined by those of heaven's host (the *Gloria*). (5) Our prayers let go, relinquishing ourselves to God (the *Nunc dimittis*).

Prayer is as relational with God as conversation is with our neighbors. We are all equals in prayer, all having the same access to God. Prayer requires persistence — Don't quit, God is listening! Because the world is deaf to us, we tend to expect God to be deaf to us. But God isn't silent or unlistening as we so often accuse him of being.

The community that Jesus initiated and that the Spirit is building is one of hospitality to the least, the lost, and the left-out, not of the cozy and comfortable. But the hospitality that God offers us in salvation easily becomes squeezed and small in Christian community as we filter out the unwanted and try to shape the community around ourselves. A false hospitality can easily mask a real inhospitality.

Our inhospitality is actually a rejection on our part of God's hospitality. Not including others actually excludes us.

An open heart requires an open home. It is difficult but essential to break down barriers to hospitality. All are invited to follow Jesus. All are included.

But if hospitality is what we are to extend to the world, it's not what we expect from the world. We expect the same treatment Jesus, Paul, and the rest received: trials. Interestingly, though, Jesus and Paul gave little attention to their trials and the power players behind them. Paying too much attention to the Herods of the world always gets the community of Jesus off track.

Resurrection completely changes the way we think about and face opposition, disappointment, and failure. There is always life on the other side of death, of crucifixion, that doesn't just get in the way but is in fact the way itself of the gospel. Resurrection means ultimate success, no matter what the current conditions are like.

"Learning how to live as the community of Christ is largely a matter of becoming familiar with and disciplined to the means by which the Father, Son, and Holy Spirit work formationally among us: namely, by the Holy Spirit from God's side and prayerful obedience from ours, by hospitably including the unwanted outsiders of the world into the community, and by cultivating a detachment from the world's insiders and their ways, especially as these ways are exemplified in the leaders and celebrities" (p. 299).

Quotations to Consider

"The story of Jesus doesn't end with Jesus. It continues in the community of the men and women who repent, believe, and follow" (p. 267).

"There is nothing in a Holy Spirit–conceived life that exempts that life from the common lot of humanity" (p. 269).

". . . what the community does and says and prays is continuous with what Jesus does and says and prays. This is the same Jesus story that we read in the Gospel but without Jesus being visibly and audibly present. The Holy Spirit is God's way of being present and active among us in the same way that he was in Jesus" (p. 270).

"The power of God is always exercised in personal ways, creating and saving and blessing. It is never an impersonal application of force from without" (p. 272).

"The moment the community exercises power apart from the story of Jesus, tries to manipulate people or events in ways that short-circuit personal relationships and intimacies, we can be sure it is not the power of the Holy Spirit; it is the devil's work. The Holy Spirit, no matter how loudly or frequently or piously invoked in such settings, is a stranger to such religious blasphemies" (p. 272).

"Prayer begins when God addresses us. First God speaks; our response, our answer, is prayer: we never initiate prayer, even though we think we do" (p. 273).

"However earthbound we feel, however humdrum and mundane our work is (shepherding in that society was equivalent to bagging groceries in ours), our prayers give us a place in a choir that expresses all the melodies and harmonies that heaven comprises" (p. 275).

We are all "equals, peers with identical access to the ear, the attention, the consideration of God" (p. 277).

"Especially if we are used to being ignored . . . get used to being listened to by God" (p. 277).

". . . the conditions necessary for prayer: a desperate, gut sense of need and a heart sense that God is the only one who can do anything about it. Prayer is not casual. Prayer is not a whimsical nod upward. Prayer is urgent, nothing less than a life-and-death matter . . ." (p. 278).

"To suppose that if we can just 'place' Christian men and women in prominent positions of leadership, we are going to improve the efficacy of the community in its worship, missions, or evangelism, has no warrant in Scripture or history" (p. 289).

"It is more than curious that the Jesus community continues to court Herod-like people in hopes of gaining their approval, recruiting them as allies, and using their influence in the cause of the kingdom" (p. 294).

"The World is a seductive place. Once we begin to cater to its interests, appeal to its curiosities, shape our language to its idioms and syntax, embrace its criteria of relevance, we abandon our basic orientation" (p. 295).

". . . once resurrection is introduced into the story, all the ways in which we work have to be rethought, re-imagined, and reworked. The world's means can no longer be employed for kingdom ends" (p. 298).

Questions for Interaction

1. "Power" is a key word in the book of Acts. Look at the following passages in Acts to consider how the words "power" and "powerful" are used — 1:8; 3:12; 4:7, 28, 33; 6:8; 7:22; 8:10; 9:22; 10:38; 13:17; 19:20; 26:18. Discuss how this power is different from the way the world uses its power. (You may or may not want to consider other power-type words. Signs and wonders — 2:22, 43; 4:30; 5:12; 6:8; 7:36; 14:3; 15:12. Strong — 3:7, 16. Strength — 9:19. Weak — 20:35.)
2. How is power used in your workplace? Your home? Your church?
3. Is there any part of your life that feels unprayable? What part of your day-to-day life have you not mentioned to God for a long time, even years?
4. The entire book of Acts turns on the prayers of the community. How significant is prayer in your small group? church? family? individual life? (Note: Praying isn't just alone or just in community; it's both.)
5. In Luke-Acts, the "outsiders" of that culture — women, Samaritans, Gentiles, tax collectors, prostitutes, "sinners" — are constantly being welcomed into the company of Jesus and the community of the church. Who are the outsiders of our culture? How welcome are they in your church? Your home?

6. What is the difference between being a welcoming community and being an inviting community?

7. Jesus mostly ignored the politicians of his time. Paul neither ignored nor put his hope in the civil institutions and governments as he went about his mission. How much hope do you place on the actions of government to save the world and serve the church?

8. What things and possibilities does the World "offer" that tempt you to cater to it?

9. Unsuccessful in court, rejected by his own people, and in chains, Paul and the gospel prevail — unhindered! What images of success hinder the gospel in you? How might you be "released" to be "unhindered" in your gospel witness?

10. What opposition or disappointment or failure are you facing and what would it mean to trust the God who raised Jesus from the dead in it? To pray in it? To obey in it?

Prayers

Use the five prayers in Luke 1–2 as a guide to your praying together. Read one of them and allow time following it for one or more in your group to pray in the same spirit. It is very appropriate for these to be personal, named prayers.

> The *Fiat mihi* — Luke 1:38
> The *Magnificat* — Luke 1:46-55
> The *Benedictus* — Luke 1:68-79
> The *Gloria* — Luke 2:14
> The *Nunc dimittis* — Luke 2:29-32

SESSION 14

Christ Plays in Community (4)

(pp. 300-338)

Summary

There are right ways and wrong ways to try to do the same thing, and that's especially true of Christian community. We can try to bypass the community of Jesus with talent and technique, avoid it as spectators, or interfere with it by trying to take over. But the "focal practice for cultivating fear-of-the-Lord in community is baptism that achieves mature formation in the practice of love" (p. 301).

Baptism shapes not just what we do, but how we do it.

The first aspect of baptism which teaches us how to live in community is its triune nature. Baptized into the Trinity, we discover that community must be personal, just as the Father, Son, and Holy Spirit are personal both with each other and with us. In a culture that treats us as functions, we must retain this personal identity.

Second, baptism engages us in what God is doing in the world. While God invites us to participate, that doesn't mean that he stops doing things. We are not the hands and feet of God. We add ours to his, but we never replace God.

Third, baptism draws us into mystery. God is bigger than our thoughts of him and so is the community of Jesus. Therefore, our primary approach to God is worship, not work.

Because the way of God is so different from the way of the world, we start by repenting, changing direction. And then we move forward again, but this time following Jesus. Watching him, obeying him, and praying to him keep us moving in the right direction. When we're follow-ing Jesus, we're paying much more attention to him than to ourselves or the world.

With baptism shaping who we are, love is what we do. The First Epistle of John is our training ground in love. In it, John doesn't just tell his readers to love, he loves us in the way he writes to us. Love is first. All else follows, flowing out of it.

Love never ends. It is never achieved. It is never checked off the list. It is our on-going requirement as a community. Not only is it never ac-complished, but it always comes out flawed. Not only are we influenced wrongly by the culture outside of us, but we deconstruct love by the sin that comes from inside us.

If we don't acknowledge that we are a community of baptized sin-ners, we will either (a) settle for appearances, which basically turns us into a moral club, or (b) get angry and mean. "It is the forgiveness of sin that frees men and women to love, and in that freedom, commands them to love" (p. 315).

We can't get to love until we deal with sin. When we finally focus on love, we will have focused on sin. If we want to feel good in our loving, we need to feel bad in our sinning. These two always go together.

We have schools to remedy ignorance, political processes to rem-edy weakness, businesses to remedy lack of money, medicine to rem-edy illness, and courts to remedy injustice — all of them are good solu-tions to real problems. But none of them deals with sin, our biggest problem.

One of the main ways we avoid loving real people is by avoiding the flesh and blood Jesus. "A dehumanized Jesus allows us to develop a prac-tice of love that has nothing to do with actual people" (p. 323). John calls people who believe and live this way antichrists.

John's community was struggling with the departure of a group of people from them. A dehumanized theology of Jesus led them to dehu-manize and depart from the community. They were more interested in a perfect church than forgiving the people of the baptized church.

Christian love isn't just a good idea or an important suggestion, it is commanded of us. Refusing to love is actually equal to murder. We learn to love by being loved ourselves by God, by seeing God's love for us in Je-sus. So, we enter the way of Jesus, the way of love, by going the way of the cross and loving others.

Key Terms

Sin: ". . . sin is basically a depersonalizing word or act. It is not, in essence, breaking a rule, but breaking a relationship. . . . Sin is a refused relationship with God that spills over into a wrong relationship with others — it is personal or it is nothing" (p. 316).

Antichrist: Anyone who denies the humanity of Jesus, preferring a more spiritual but ultimately abstract Christ.

Perfectionism: "The denial of sin and the accompanying programs or strategies to develop a way of life that is indifferent to or marginalizes sin . . ." (p. 320).

Quotations to Consider

". . . the defining first act and word marking life in the community of the resurrection is holy baptism" (p. 302).

"The fact is that when we are studied like specimens in a laboratory, what is learned is on the level of what is learned from an autopsy. The only way to know another is in a personal relationship, and that involves at least minimal levels of trust and risk" (p. 304).

"God is totally personal, *inter*personal, relational, giving and receiving, loving and directing" (p. 304).

"God is not an undefined sort of energy or function in place somewhere waiting for us to show up with the right technique or the correct password to swing him into action. He is already active, enormously and incessantly active, creating and saving, healing and blessing, forgiving and judging" (p. 305).

The mystery of God "is not a mystery that keeps us in the dark, but a mystery in which we are taken by the hand and gradually led into the light, a light to which our souls are not yet accustomed" (p. 306).

"God is never a commodity that we can use . . ." (p. 307).

". . . love is not an item in a catalogue available on order to Christians; it is

68

the way of life that permeates and sums up the thinking and behavior of followers of Jesus in the company of the Trinity" (p. 310).

"Anyone who joins a church expecting to be part of a happy and harmonious gathering of put-together people sooner or later is in for serious disappointment" (p. 311).

"Men and women are not admitted to the community by presenting credentials of love skills, nor do we maintain our place in the community by passing periodic peer reviews on love. We are here to be formed over our lifetimes into a community of the beloved, God's beloved who are being formed into a people who love God and one another in the way and on the terms in which God loves us. It's slow work" (p. 312).

"The people with whom we live in community are all sinners, every last one of them" (p. 315).

". . . we will never get love right if we don't get sin right, and the looming difficulty in getting sin right is our propensity to deny or minimize it" (p. 316).

"A refusal to deal with sin is a refusal to deal with relationships. And if we don't deal with relationships, we can't love" (p. 316).

"The only place, quite literally the only place, where sin is taken seriously in community, is the Christian community, the congregation" (pp. 318-19).

"At the core of who we are, there is something wrong, something wrong relationally, wrong personally between us and our neighbors and God. The only way to deal with it is by forgiveness" (p. 319).

"Sin confessed and forgiven frees us to develop relationships of love with our Lord and with one another" (p. 321).

"Our identity as the beloved of God allows no other way of life than that of loving others" (p. 321).

"Loving a dehumanized Jesus means loving in a way that has nothing to do with anything particular men and woman are doing in our community. We become lovers of ideas and feelings, lovers of ecstasy and novelty," not of God (p. 323).

"Sin reduces the people around us to roles or objects so that we can use them or manipulate them or condescendingly help them. They are depersonalized so that we don't have to be relational with them" (p. 324).

"This is who you are, your identity, *loved by God*. But being loved is not all there is to it. Being loved creates a person who can love, who *must* love. Getting love is a launch into giving love" (p. 328).

"Only when we do the Jesus truth in the Jesus way do we get the Jesus life" (p. 334).

"We cannot participate in God's work but then insist on doing it in our own way" (p. 335).

Questions for Interaction

1. Is the American church shaped more by numbers-motivated marketing techniques or by baptism? In which ways are you and your community shaped by both?
2. Our unbaptized society treats us as numbers and colors and types and target markets instead of as persons. How has this affected the way you interact with other people? The way you think about yourself? God?
3. Looking back over the past few years, are you becoming more relational or more functional? What sort of interactions do you have with your bank teller, pastor, waitress, deacon, grocery clerk?
4. "Love" is our most important and most abused word. What is real love like? How do you know it, recognize it?
5. When we feel the need for change in our communities, which do we change first: our committees, our music, our leadership, or our hearts? Why?
6. Which is easier: to ignore sin or to forgive sin? Why?
7. Have you ever been a part of a Christian community that was honest about sin and thereby learned love? Have you ever been a part of one that chose perfectionism over honesty? Describe your experience.
8. How does fanciful literature about an apocalyptic Antichrist keep

us from seeing the antichrists around us — those who deny the humanity of Jesus?

9. How is commanded love stronger than love that arises from feelings?
10. Why is the refusal to love equated with murder?
11. How does Jesus' loving us enable us to love others?

Prayers

The well-known passage in Scripture that we return to repeatedly to learn and relearn love is 1 Corinthians 13:4-8a. Pray through each of the phrases of this passage one at a time, adding in the details of your lives and the life of your community as you do. You may want to assign the phrases to people in the group or leave time open between the reading of each one for anyone in the group to pray silently or aloud.

> Love is patient;
> love is kind;
> love is not envious
> or boastful
> or arrogant
> or rude.
> It does not insist on its own way;
> it is not irritable or resentful;
> it does not rejoice in wrongdoing,
> but rejoices in the truth.
> It bears all things,
> believes all things,
> hopes all things,
> endures all things.
> Love never ends.